the handmade basket book

rebecca board

Dedicated with love to my mother, Wendy.

First published in the United States in 2002 by

krause publications

700 East State Street • Iola, WI 54990-0001
715/445-2214 • FAX: 715/445-4087   www.krause.com

ISBN 0-87349-387-7

Editor: Claire Waite-Brown
Senior Editor: Clare Hubbard
Design and Art Direction: Blackjacks
Photographer: Emma Peios
Editorial Direction: Rosemary Wilkinson

Reproduction by Modern Age Repro House Ltd, Hong Kong
Printed and bound in Singapore by Tien Wah Press

Every effort has been made to present clear and accurate instructions. Therefore, the author and
publishers can offer no guarantee or accept any liability for any injury, illness or damage which
may inadvertently be caused to the user while following these instructions.

Library of Congress Catalog Number: 2001095625

ACKNOWLEDGMENTS

Thanks are due to the following people: Ian Sidaway for the beautiful illustrations; Peter and Jenny
for lending me the computer and Paul for showing me how it works; Katy for helping me out at
the last minute with all those plaited rushes.

contents

introd

For many years now I have been delighting in the treasures that nature has to offer. I hope that this book will inspire you to consider a field to be like a fairy's thread shop and a hedgerow like a goldmine.

I have filled the following pages with as many different basketmaking ideas as possible. First of all there are details of a diverse range of raw materials including willow, rushes, grasses and leaves. The skills needed to weave these into wreaths, mats and baskets are then explained through a series of projects. All this combines to give a close-up insight into the world of basketmaking so that with a little experience you may be inspired to adapt the projects and design your own work.

You need to be fairly intuitive when working with natural materials, as they are all different and their character and pliability are affected by soil type and weather conditions. For that reason treat the notes I have written on preparation as guidelines only, they are there to help you get to know your materials. Once you've grasped the basics, this book will provide you with a valuable range of sound technical advice with which to enjoy making your own creations from whatever you have on your doorstep. You may find that you get totally involved and start planting your garden with leaves and stems specially for their weavability. Growing and gathering your own materials helps you to understand them better and enables you to reflect the rhythms of the seasons in the weaves of your basket. Always remember, however, to make sure any material you gather from the wild is not rare or endangered.

uction

raw materials

The following pages will advise you on growing, gathering and getting to grips with the different materials you can use to weave, plait and coil baskets and mats.

farmed willow

The Latin name for willow is *Salix* and the shoots are harvested annually by being cut almost at ground level. Particular varieties are used for basketmaking because they have characteristics that make them "kind," which means they are comparatively willing to be woven into baskets.

❑ *Salix triandra* are good, all-purpose willows. **Black Maul** is the variety most often grown commercially, and it can be bought stripped or unstripped (see below).

❑ *Salix purpurea* are fine, tough willows suitable for detailed, refined work.

❑ *Salix viminalis* are stout, coarse willows traditionally used for agricultural work. They include some of the super willows which can grow up to 10 feet in a year and are suitable to be used for making large-scale structures.

❑ **Flanders Red** is another variety used for basketmaking. It is characterized by its wonderful rusty color.

Willow is sold in bundles according to height, ranging from 3 to 8 feet. You can also buy bundles of thicker, two-year growth sticks for handles, square work and larger structures. The taller the willow the thicker its diameter at the base of the rod. Having said that, any given bundle contains a variety of different thicknesses as it is a natural material and no two rods are exactly the same. The basket maker has to select the thickness required by eye.

Willow for basketmaking is available direct from the growers. Most growers will supply "beginners' bundles," which contain willow rods of assorted heights.

Farmed willow is available in the following forms, chosen for their colors and different working qualities:

❑ **Stripped willow**, predominantly Black Maul, has had the bark removed. There are two types: **white willow** and **buff willow**. To produce white willow, bundles of rods are "pitted" – left standing in water until they are just coming into leaf. At this point the bark is loose and can easily be stripped off. In the past this was done by pulling each rod through a willow brake, a two-pronged piece of metal a bit like a tuning fork. Nowadays the process is mechanized and the willow can be stripped much more quickly, a handful at a time. To produce buff willow, the rods are first boiled and then stripped. During the process tannin in the willow's bark stains the wood a warm orangey-brown.

❑ **Unstripped willow** has not had the bark removed. Instead, the willow is harvested and dried and so retains its natural color – usually green. Unstripped willow is rather confusingly known as "brown" whatever the hue of its bark. If you were to ask a willow grower for "green" wood you would be given newly gathered willow, that is still pliable and sappy. **Steamed willow**, however, has been treated; boiled in water until the bark goes dark brown or sometimes almost black.

From left to right: wild willow, purpurea "Welsh strain", Flanders Red, triandra "whissender", bundles of mixed stems of purpurea, triandra Black Maul and stripped willow.

preparing farmed willow

Willow should be stored in a dry environment. This could be a shed or barn or a dark, dry corner in the house. In order to preserve the color of the wood it should be kept out of bright sunlight (white willow will become a warmer gold color and some of the greens will soften on prolonged exposure to light). The wood will keep indefinitely, but watch out for woodworm.

Before use, bought farmed willow needs to be soaked in cold water until it becomes pliable. This can be done in a cattle trough, bath, pond, or stream.

Completely submerge the material and weigh it down well with stones. The taller sizes are the thickest and need to be in the water longest. The table below will give you an idea of how long the wood needs to soak.

You can speed up the process by using warm water. When the willow is soaked, mellow it by letting it lie wrapped up in damp sacking for 1 hour if stripped or overnight if unstripped. From my own experience, I find that Flanders Red usually needs to be in the water slightly longer than other varieties.

soaking times

	Stripped Willow	Unstripped Willow
3 to 4 feet	Approx. 1 hour	Approx. 3–4 days
5 to 6 feet	Approx. 2 hours	Approx. 5 days
7 feet and above	Approx. 3 hours	Approx. 6–7 days

hedgerow woods

As well as all the beautiful stems you may find, this category includes the usable woods of some garden shrubs and trees whose shoots are long, pliable and reasonably branch-free. Anything that has slender, first year growth and is flexible enough to bend around your wrist without snapping can be used for basketmaking. Choose woods that have an attractive color, texture or scent. The options are endless and there is always something new to discover, so keep your eyes open

and your pruners handy. Always ask permission before gathering materials from someone else's land.

As a very general rule it is best to use a pliable wood, such as a willow or dogwood, for the side stakes of your basket and incorporate the less co-operative woods into the side weaving. Parking lots around supermarkets and business parks are often planted with a fiesta of brightly colored willows and dogwoods. They are a great source of cuttings or even an entire harvest, if you are lucky enough to catch the landscape gardener who looks after them.

Other good basketmaking materials include honeysuckle, wisteria, bright green winter jasmine, privet, snowberry, any of the ornamental willows, spiraea, vines, forsythia and shrubby germander. This last plant has interesting white stems but it is evergreen, so you will need to pick the leaves off. Avoid elder, apple tree prunings and the type of ivy that grows against walls, since these are too snappy to weave with.

Pliable shoots and twigs can also be harvested. You can use twigs from the alder tree, with its blue-violet buds and catkins in January, and the young brown shoots of hornbeam, sprinkled with snowy white dots.

Hedgerow and garden materials from left to right: ivy, privet, salix arbutifolia, shrubby germander and hazel twigs with catkins.

Right: *Hedgerow materials, from left to right: ornamental willow – salix alba vitellina, spindle, cultivated dogwood, ash, hazel, wild rose and lime.*

Bottom to top: Flanders Red, ivy, field maple, ash, hazel twigs, willow variety Flanders Red, willow variety arbutifolia, alder with violet buds, thin strip of honeysuckle, willow variety alba vitellina and, just showing, border in willow variety Flanders Red.

Bottom to top: field maple, hazel, privet, wild willow and willow variety Flanders Red.

Balsam poplar is great for its deep brown stems and honey scent. Lime is one of my favorite woods. The usable shoots grow around the base of the tree or sprout from the top if it has been pollarded. The wood has a shaky character with plenty of buds and ranges in color from green and gold at the base to deep red at the tip. It is the basketry equivalent of handspun wool. Watch out though – lime does shrink when dried out. Eucalyptus, weeping willow, beech and holly are also worth looking for.

Wild woods suitable for weaving with include hazel, ash, wild willow, dogwood, oak, spindle, field maple, hanging ivy, brambles, blackthorn, wild rose and elm.

growing willow

To grow your own willow, prepare and plant in winter. Simply cut stout 9-inch lengths from freshly gathered rods and push them into well-prepared earth (i.e. dug over and thoroughly weeded) a couple of feet apart. Make sure there are a couple of buds showing above the ground. Weed around the plants, especially in the first few years while they are establishing themselves, to make sure they don't get engulfed. Planting through sheets of black polythene or fabric mulch (available from garden

Left: Hedgerow, garden and woodland materials, including wild honeysuckle, whitebeam, cultivated dogwood, coppiced alder, wisteria and alder tree twigs.

centers) is worth considering to help with weed control.

Harvest the shoots that grow every winter. You won't get much at the end of the first year, but by about the third season you will have a reasonable crop. Once gathered, let your willow dry out in the shelter of an airy shed or porch. Then, tie it in bundles, store it and soak it when you need it.

If you don't have access to a plant from which to take cuttings, you will have to go to a specialist supplier (see List of Suppliers on page 78).

ornamental willows

All kinds of willow are worth growing, particularly some of the ornamental varieties such as orange *Salix alba*, and violet *Salix daphniodes*, for their interesting characters and colorful stems. Ornamental willows are best prepared in the same way as hedgerow woods to preserve the colors, buds and bloom.

gathering hedgerow woods

Gather woods at the end of autumn through to the beginning of spring when the sap is down, the leaves have fallen and the year's growth is complete. You will need to strip the thorns off brambles by pulling them through a thick leather gardening glove, peel the leaves off evergreen woods such as privet and ivy and pick the thorns off wild rose and sloe.

preparing hedgerow woods

If you weave the materials immediately after gathering, while they are still green, you will build a basket that is rigid at first, but loosens and becomes rickety as it dries out. To get around this problem it is necessary to let the woods shrink first by leaving them outside, tied in bundles, under the shelter of a bush or shrub for about three weeks, depending on the species. This process allows the rods to wilt and shrink without completely drying out and losing their pliability. They are then ready to weave. It is alright to let them get covered with snow or rain but they should be protected from the sun and wind. Don't put anything over the top of them. Drying and re-soaking hedgerow woods is not really recommended as they often lose their lovely colors.

center cane

This is a natural material, though you might think otherwise on account of its very even nature and lack of color variation. This very familiar and widely used basketmaking material is the central, pithy core of the rattan plant, a climbing tropical creeper that grows wild in Southeast Asia. It has a thorny outer bark that enables it to support itself by climbing other trees in the forest. Having reached its maximum width, it neither branches nor expands, it just keeps on growing upwards towards the light above the forest canopy. After harvesting, the thorny bark is removed and the hard outer skin is peeled off and used as chair cane and glossy lapping cane or wrapping cane. The former is used for weaving cane seats on chairs and the latter is used to bind joints on cane furniture and basket handles and rims.

The central pith is then processed into even lengths of flat band and circular canes. Ribbons of flat band cane look like tagliatelli pasta and can be used for wrapping handles and for the side weaving on stake and strand and frame baskets.

Center cane is easy to work and has the great advantage of taking up dye very readily. It is processed into strands with a circular diameter (like spaghetti) and is available in a variety of sizes from 000 to 15. Thicker, handle cane is also available. Center cane is widely used for weaving stake and strand and frame baskets and is also good as a core for wrapped coiled baskets.

preparing center cane

THIRTY MINUTES BEFORE USE: Soak the cane in hot water until it is pliable enough to use. This will take about 30 minutes for the thicker material and just a quick dip for the thinnest. Don't leave it in the water for hours on end or it will discolor. Any unused cane can be dried out and resoaked at a later date. Center cane can be dried out by letting it air at room temperature; it should then be stored in a dry place.

Examples of cane and raffia; clockwise from top left hand corner: glossy lapping cane, center cane, flat band cane and raffia.

raffia

Raffia is taken from the underside of the leaves of the palm *Raphia ruffia,* which grows in Madagascar. It can be used dry for coiling and dyes well. Raffia is available from craft shops and garden centers. It should be stored in a dry place, but it needs no special preparation.

garden leaves

Many garden leaves can be used for coiled work, and some of the larger, broader ones can be plaited or woven too.

preparing garden leaves

Look for tall, straight leaves from plants such as iris, day lily, red hot poker, ginger lily, montbretia, New Zealand flax and gladioli, and harvest them when they are fully grown. For the majority of plants this will be just after they have finished flowering. Spread the leaves out to dry on sheets of newspaper in an airy room and turn them frequently.

STORING GARDEN LEAVES: Tie dried leaves in loose bundles that should be kept somewhere where they won't get damp, until needed.

THREE TO TWELVE HOURS BEFORE USE: Sprinkle the leaves with water, turn them to distribute the moisture and wrap them up in damp fabric for a few hours until pliable. I find that some leaves, such as day lily, become pliable very quickly, whereas gladioli leaves need to be left overnight or longer. Don't leave them submerged in water or they will saturate like a sponge and the resulting basket will be loose when dried.

grasses

Grasses make very good cores for coiled work, both wrapped and exposed. They should be used as dry as possible, otherwise they will shrink and result in a loosely woven basket. Grasses can also be used to add decoration to a basket.

preparing grasses

Gather grasses during summer, early on, before the seedheads are fully open, or they will shed. Dry grasses by spreading them on sheets of newspaper or a wire rack in an airy room, turning them frequently.

STORING GRASSES: Store wrapped in newspaper or hanging up in bundles, making sure they are out of direct sunlight in order to preserve their colors.

lavender

Lavender stalks are an excellent material for coiling to make scented as well as decorative baskets.

preparing lavender

Harvest lavender on a warm, sunny day when the buds are a good color, but still tightly closed. Set to work in the morning, after the dew has evaporated, as the essential oils will be at their strongest then. If you are going to strip the leaves, do this carefully on the same day. Tie the lavender in bundles and hang it up to dry in an airy room away from direct sunlight.

STORING LAVENDER: Wrap the lavender in newspaper or put it in a lidded cardboard box and store it in a dry, dark place.

TWO HOURS BEFORE USE: Submerge the lavender bundles in a sinkful of warm water and leave to soak for about two hours. The lavender is ready to use when it will bend without snapping.

A selection of field grasses, leaves and straw, from left to right: ginger lily leaves and seed heads, species of brome, straw, gladiolus leaves, sweet vernal grass, crocisma leaves, "cock's foot" grass, day lily leaves and rough meadow grass.

rushes

Scirpus lacustris or the common bulrush grows in slow-moving rivers and streams and around lakes, often in deep water.

preparing rushes

Rushes are available to buy from specialist suppliers (see page 78), but should you wish to gather your own, here is how it is done. Rushes are ready for gathering in June, when the reddish-brown flowers show and the harvest can continue throughout the summer. The clumps should be gathered on alternate years so that the plant has a chance to rest. Cut rushes as close to their roots as possible, and handle with care since they will be very brittle at this stage. Dry them out thoroughly in a cool shed or barn for about three weeks.

STORING RUSHES: To store dried rushes, tie them in bundles and keep them out of the damp and in the dark to preserve their amazing lime green color. Exposure to light will fade them to gold, which can be just as beautiful.

THREE HOURS BEFORE USE: Sprinkle the dried rushes with a hose or watering can, turn them to spread the moisture and leave to mellow under damp sacking for about three hours. They need to be just wet enough to be soft and pliable, and should feel like ribbon. Don't leave them to soak submerged in water or they will saturate like a sponge, and you will not only have a soggy time making your basket, but it will also shrink badly and become loose when the water dries out.

IMMEDIATELY BEFORE USE: Pull each rush through a damp cloth to flatten it, clean it and expel air.

straw

Straw is useful as a core material in coiled work. Traditionally it is used for the coiled backs of Orkney chairs and bee hives. Use dry. Straw is available from specialist suppliers (see page 78).

Scirpus lacustris, the common bulrush, harvested from the River Ouse, England.

recycled materials

There are endless possibilities for basketwork using recycled materials. Keep an open mind, and, as a general rule, look for long, strong, pliable materials. You could cut up or twist polyethylene bags as a coiling material and wire is also a possibility. I once wove a bundle of galvanized electrical cable into a basket made of center cane dyed blue, and it looked like the sea.

In South Africa night watchmen developed a tradition of weaving very fine, brightly coloured telephone wire into baskets with interesting patterns. These baskets are becoming rarer as new technologies and digital phones are introduced. Some Japanese baskets contain recycled bamboo from the rafters of traditional farmhouses. These have an attractive, deep, reddish-brown color brought about by exposure to soot and smoke from cooking and other household activities.

Strips of paper and card are great for plaiting, and cut up textiles, strings and cords can be used for coiling and twining. The great thing about most recycled materials is that they can be used dry.

tools and terms

Happily, the tools needed for basketmaking are as simple and uncomplicated as the materials themselves. Most of them can be found in the home or at a hardware shop or garden center, but for one or two particular tools you will need to visit a basketmaking supplier (see page 78). As you work through the projects, refer back to these pages if there is a tool or term you are unfamiliar with.

tools

BASKETMAKER'S BODKIN: A metal spike with a wooden handle, used for opening up a space in the weaving and for prodding the stakes to show them where to bend.

FLORIST'S WIRE: For binding decorations onto a wreath and holding together the first few elements of a random weave basket.

HOOP: A circle made of a few long twisted willow rods can be used to hold your stakes upright. Alternatively, you can tie them up with string. Make your own hoop by winding about three long branch-free willow rods into a circle. This is done in the same way as hazel is wound into a wreath (see page 20).

KNIFE: Either a craft knife or a traditional curved basketmaker's knife can be used for slyping stakes – cutting on the diagonal – and cleaving and shaving skeins. The knife must be sharp.

LARGE-EYED NEEDLE: For stitching plaited rushes and coiled work.

On the left, top to bottom: scissors, rapping iron, rush threader, basketmaker's bodkin, traditional curved basketmaking knife, wooden mold.

On the right, clockwise: paintbrush, large smooth stone, linen thread, water spray, pruners, craft knife, florist's wire. Center: pliers.

METAL RULER: To measure your work.

MOLD: Plaited baskets sometimes need to be woven over a mold and woven rush baskets are almost always made over a mold, such as a cardboard box or cake tin.

PAINTBRUSH: For varnishing cane and cardboard.

PLIERS: Used to help pull the needle through stitched plaited rushwork and some coiled work.

PRUNERS: Used for cutting out material, harvesting woods and pruning finished baskets.

RAPPING IRON: For beating down weaving in willow work to make it dense and close up the gaps.

ROUND-NOSED PLIERS: Used to squeeze center cane to make it bend in a specific place.

RUSH THREADER: Use this tool to thread the ends of rushes through existing weaving.

SACKING: Use damp sacking to mellow willow (see page 8). This is a hessian sack of the type used to hold grain etc. Pet shops or seed merchants may provide used sacking or you can buy hessian from fabric and department stores.

SCISSORS: for tidying up rushwork.

STONES: For weighting down a basket during weaving.

TROUGH: A galvanized metal trough is useful for soaking willow in, or improvise by using a bath, pond or stream.

WATER SPRAY: Spray your stakes and weavers regularly to stop them drying out and becoming brittle.

a useful glossary of terms

BACK: The outside of the natural curve on a willow rod.
BELLY: The inside of the natural curve on a willow rod.
BORDER: Interlacement of stakes round a basket's rim.

BROWN WILLOW: This refers to dried unstripped willow, whatever its hue.
BUTT: The thick end of a rod or rush.
CHAIN PAIRING: A weave created by working alternate rows of pairing and reverse pairing.
CHECKWEAVE: Under one, over one plaiting weave used in rushwork.
CLEAVE: To split or separate a willow rod into skeins.
ENGLISH RAND: In front of one, behind one weave.
FITCHING: Weave used after a band of openwork.
FRAME BASKET: Basket woven over a framework of wooden hoops.
GREEN WOOD: Newly gathered wood.
HANDLE BOW: The structural rod of a handle.
HANDLE LINERS: Sticks to mark a channel for the handle bow.
LAZY SQUAW STITCH: Basic wrapped coiling stitch.
NAVAJO STITCH: Coiling stitch where the core is covered twice.
OPENWORK: Commonly used in French basketry, the stakes or uprights are usually held together with a fitching weave.
PACKING: Building up a specific area of weaving by working back and forth over a group of stakes.
PAIRING: A weave using two weavers, often used on bases. The twist in the weave appears to slope upwards slightly.
PICKING OFF: Cutting the unwanted ends off a completed basket.
REVERSE PAIRING: Pairing with the twist in the opposite direction. The twist in the weave appears to slope downwards slightly.
SCALLOM: Long tongue cut on the end of a willow rod.
SKEIN: A thin band or ribbon of split willow.
SLEW: In and out weave using two or more strands.
SLYPE: Diagonal cut on the end of a rod.
STAKES: Upright rods round the sides of a basket.
STAKING UP: Inserting the side stakes of a basket.
TIP: Thin end of a rod or rush.
TRAC: A type of border.
TYING IN THE SLATH: Weaving round the interlaced base sticks on a round or oval basket.
UPSETT: Dense weave around the base of a basket.
WALE: Weave with three or more strands twining round the stakes.
WEAVER: Strand of material for weaving with.

proje

The following array of projects will enable you to see a wide range of basketry techniques and materials in context. Within each section – random weaving, stake and strand, frame, plaiting and coiling – the projects are arranged in order of difficulty with the easiest first. If you are new to willow basketmaking, I strongly recommend that you complete the Wreath (pages 20 to 21) and the Bread Basket (pages 22 to 27) projects first, as these will help you become accustomed to using the tools and materials and familiarize you with basketmaking terms.

Weaving with natural materials is utterly absorbing and your friends and family may have to move over to make space for some bundles of twigs, but they're bound not to mind as the house starts to fill up with delightful new baskets, mats, cake racks and wreaths that you have made yourself. Always soak a few spare willow rods just in case of mishaps and natural surprises such as snapping, peeling and cracking in unlikely places. Read through each project carefully before you start and look up any unfamiliar terms in the glossary (see page 17). If you are left-handed and prefer to weave in the opposite direction, viewing the diagrams with the book propped up in front of a mirror may be helpful.

cts

practising simple random weaving is a great way to get used to
handling and manipulating the raw materials of basketmaking. It is
a very free and easy method of basketmaking with virtually no rules.
Think of a bird building a nest. It can be as simple or complex, rough
and ready or fine and delicate as you like.

random weave
hazel wreath

In winter, when hazel is silvery and covered with tiny buds, it can be gathered and twisted into a
Christmas wreath. If you wait until spring you can make one with catkins on. Alternatively, ivy,
wisteria or any other long, pliable stems could be twisted to form the basis of this project, instead of
hazel. Throughout the year save leaves, dried flowers and other natural finds with which to decorate
your wreath. Ferns and oak leaves sprayed silver and gold look particularly good.

raw materials
4 hazel rods or branches, about $\frac{1}{3}$–$\frac{1}{2}$ inch diameter at the base and
   $5\frac{1}{2}$ feet long, with plenty of twiggy side shoots, especially near the
   top. You will need to use them immediately, while they are
   still pliable.
Leaves and flowers for decoration, such as bay leaves and dried
   hydrangea flowers

other essentials
Pruners
Basketmaker's bodkin
Florists' wire

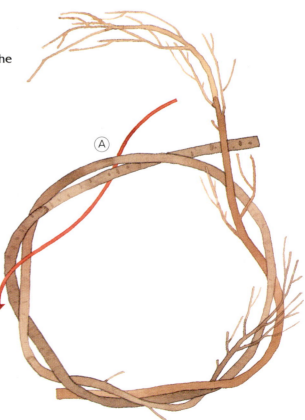

1 Ease one of the hazel rods into a hoop shape about 15 inches
in diameter. Thread the ends of the branch round itself,
through the circle, several times until the hoop supports itself.

2 Add in another hazel rod and twine it round the first,
making sure that the butt ends of each rod are on the
underside of the hoop and opposite each other, so that the
weight of the wreath is balanced and the joins don't occur in
the same place (A). You will find that you need to bunch up the
side shoots in order to feed them through the circle.

variation

A similar technique can be used to make a random weave basket. Take a very branched, twiggy piece of hazel and form it into the skeleton of a dish, using twists of florists' wire to bind key shoots together and draw the whole thing into shape. Take a couple of clumps of weeping willow and weave them in, out and around the hazel, looping and sculpting to make a pleasing form. More florists' wire may be necessary at this stage, though it can be removed later when the structure supports itself. Add a long length of wisteria for strength, weaving it in and out of the mesh and pulling it like a drawstring through the rim of the basket to stop the soft weeping willow flopping over into a plate shape. Continue threading willow and wisteria in and out, closely interlacing them with the existing structure to make a dense and sturdy woven form. Last but not least, add in some catkins. This is just one example, obviously any selection of materials can be used.

3 Add in the last two branches with the butt ends on the underside and at regular intervals around the wreath. The self-supporting wreath can now be decorated.

4 Decide how you want to arrange your leaves and flowerheads around the wreath. Trap their stems between the twists of hazel. You may find a basketmaker's bodkin helpful here to ease a space between the branches. Fasten the decorations on with florists' wire.

variation

This wreath was decorated with mauve hydrangeas and eucalyptus leaves.

the stakes in a stake and strand basket are the thick upright rods that form the support around the side of the basket. The strands are the thinner rods that weave in and out of the stakes to fill in the sides. The base of a stake and strand basket is usually made separately, the base sticks are the thickest of all, and fine base weavers are manipulated around them. The stakes are then inserted into the base, bent up to form the basis of the sides and, eventually, worked into the final top border.

techniques practice
bread basket

Making this bread basket will familiarize you with the basic techniques of willow work. This one is made from unstripped Black Maul, but you could use any variety of willow.

raw materials
Soak and mellow the following willow (see page 8):

UNSTRIPPED BLACK MAUL WILLOW

6 base sticks, approx. 1 foot long, cut from the butt ends of the thickest rods in a 4 foot bundle

Up to 60 thin 4-foot rods for base and side weaving

25 thick 4-foot rods for the side stakes

14 medium thickness 4-foot rods for the upsett

other essentials
Basketmaker's bodkin
Knife
Water spray
Pruners
Hoop, about 11 inches in diameter
Large smooth stone to use as weight
Rapping iron

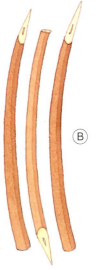

1 Place three base sticks next to each other, alternating tip and butt ends. Use a basketmaker's bodkin to pierce the center of the base sticks and leave them threaded onto the bodkin (A).

2 Use a sharp knife to slype the tip ends of the remaining three base sticks (B). A slype is a diagonal cut that makes it easier to push a rod into another rod or through a space in the weaving. Always cut away from you.

3 Thread the three slyped base sticks into the three pierced base

sticks, alternating the tip and butt ends. The willow usually has a natural curve on it. Thread your slyped base sticks so that they curve downwards. Make your base slightly domed so that it is strong and sits evenly on a surface.

4 Take two of the thin rods, evenly matched in thickness and length, and thread their tip ends into the slit in the pierced base sticks. Start to weave by bending one weaver horizontally in front of the threaded base sticks and one to the back. Bring the weaver at the back round to the front of the pierced sticks (C), and take the one at the front round to the back of the pierced sticks.

5 Turn the work after each stroke so that you keep what you're doing at the top, and weave twice around the center in this way

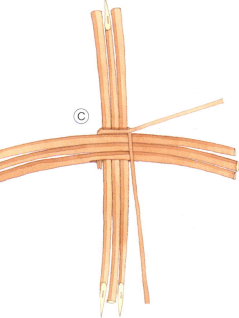

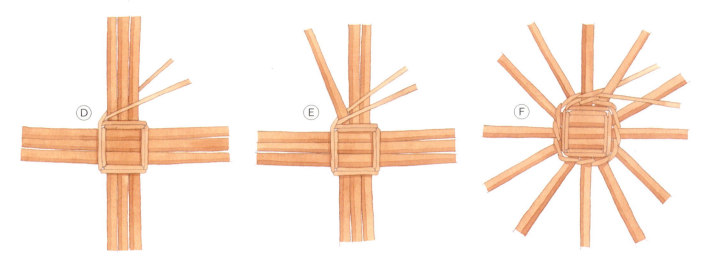

(D). The weaving should be as neat and close to the middle as possible. This process is called tying in the slath.

6 Now weave round the base sticks individually, splaying them out as you go so that you have adequate space to weave into. The weave used is called pairing and the weavers will alternately twine round the base sticks, crossing over each other. Start by bringing both the weavers to the front of the work in adjacent spaces (E). Take the weaver on the left round to the back of the work (it will pass over the top of the right-hand weaver and behind the next base stick before coming back round to the front again in the following space, see diagram C on page 47).

7 The other weaver will now be on the left and you are ready to continue weaving, repeating the sequence, trying to dome the base as you go (F). After a while you should get into a rhythm with it. Don't worry if everything isn't absolutely perfect on your first attempt, that will come with practice. Remember to spray the wood with water regularly so that it does not dry out.

8 Eventually you will need to join in a new pair of weavers. Choose two that are evenly matched in

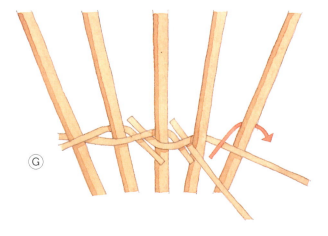

thickness and length. Always join both weavers in adjacent spaces even if one hasn't run out yet (cut the end off in this case). Join in with the butt ends when you finish with butts, and tips when you finish with tips. Starting on the left, pull the old end aside and push the new end in alongside it. Weave round the next base stick straight away, and then join in the other weaver (G). Leave the old ends sticking out for now, they can be pruned later.

9 Carry on weaving. Make sure your joins don't all occur in the same place, as this will create a weakness in the basket. You may need to make a join before the weavers have run out to achieve this. When your base measures about 8 inches in diameter, pull the tip ends of the final pair of weavers down through the previous row of weaving to secure them. Every other set of weavers will finish with tips, so if it looks as though you are going to finish with butts simply add in or take out a set, whichever leaves you with a base nearest the specified measurements. Cut off all the ends on both sides of the base using pruners. Make each cut at an angle so that they won't catch on whatever you put in the basket. Do this with care, making sure that the ends you leave are still long enough to rest on the underlying base stick, so that the weaving won't spring undone.

10 It is now time to start staking up. Take the 25 thick rods and slype each one on the back, that is the outside, of its natural curve. Push the uprights into the base with the slyped side upwards, one on each side of each base stick. This basket has straight sides, so you stake up against the curve. To give a basket curved sides, work with the curve – slype on the belly, that is the inside

of the curve and insert with the slyped sides upwards. Use your bodkin to open out the space. Insert the final (25th) stake alongside one of the others wherever they are furthest apart. Bend the uprights up against the tip of the bodkin, where they meet the base, and gather them into a hoop (H). Thread three or four uprights into the weaving of the hoop to hold it on. The hoop is a temporary measure to hold the side stakes up until there is enough side weaving in place for them to stay upright on their own (usually about four rounds). You should not rely on the hoop to hold your basket in shape. It is important to hold the stake you are weaving round at the desired angle every time you weave a stroke (that is once round the stake).

11 Now begin to weave the upsett, which is a dense band of weaving around the bottom of the basket. Two sets of weavers follow each other round, to ensure the weaving builds up evenly. Take four medium thickness rods, slype them a third of their length below the tips. Push the slyped ends into the base to the left of four consecutive uprights.

12 Lay the basket on it's side and work a four rod wale. Start with your weavers pulled down. Take the weaver on the far left in front of three uprights, behind one and back to the front again (I). Keep on repeating this stroke, using the weaver on the far left each time.

13 When you have woven halfway round the circumference of the base, slype and insert four more medium thickness rods and start them off in

exactly the same way. The two sets of weavers will follow each other round, and the weaving should cover the ends of the base sticks. When each set of weavers gets round to where the other set started, drop the rod that lands in the space where the first rod of the other set started. this is marked X on the diagram (J). Cut the dropped rod level with the bottom of the basket. Weave each of the three rods behind it for one more stroke of four rod waling.

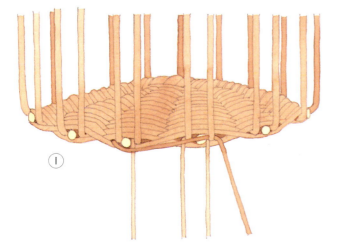

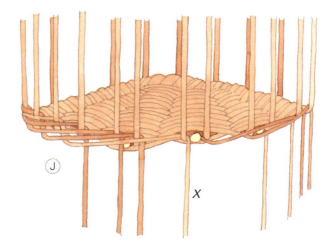

14 Now switch to three rod waling, a weave that works on the same principle as four rod waling. This time the left weaver in the group will go in front of two uprights and behind one (K). Join in new weavers butt to butt. Starting on the left, push each new weaver in alongside the old end and weave it a stroke. Join in all three weavers in a row (L). Work at gradually getting the uprights evenly spaced. This won't all happen on the first round.

15 Stand the basket upright with a rock or something heavy in it to weigh it down. Shape the basket as you go. Every time you weave a stroke hold the side stake you are weaving round at the desired angle with your left finger and thumb. The right hand maneuvers the weavers. It will not be possible to weave a good basket with willow that is too dry, so spray your weavers and uprights with water if they start to dry out.

16 Three rod wale until the basket is about $1\frac{1}{2}$ inches deep, and leave the tips on the outside. Rap the weaving down well with a rapping iron.

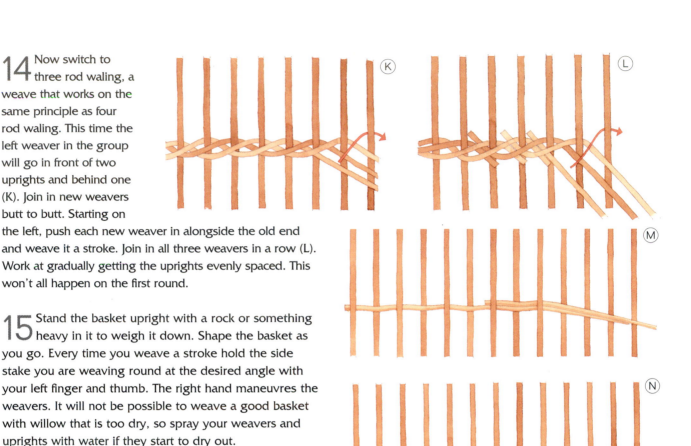

17 Now it is time to do the two rod slewing weave. This weave needs an odd number of uprights to work. If you have an even number, slype an extra rod and add it in by pushing it into the weaving alongside one of the existing stakes. Take a generous handful of the thinnest weavers and grade them into three heaps according to height. Starting with the shortest ones, take a rod and lay it in with the butt on the inside of the basket. Weave it in and out for half its length and then lay in a second weaver on top of it, again with the butt on the inside, and weave them both together, taking care that they don't get crossed over (M).

18 When the bottom weaver runs out, leave the tip on the outside, and lay in another weaver on top, with the butt on the inside (N). Keep rapping down the weaving to make it dense, and finish when the work measures about $3\frac{1}{2}$ to 4 inches. If the hoop is still in place you should now take it off. If you leave the hoop on for too long it will inhibit the weaving.

19 Now do a band of three rod wale (K) with two sets of weavers chasing each other round. Start with tip ends on opposite sides of the basket. When the weavers run out, join each set in butt to butt and weave out to the tips. Rap the weaving down so that it is level.

20 Now work a three rod border. This is a good standard border to learn first. Denser four, five, six and, if the stakes are very close together, seven rod borders can all be worked on the same principle. Make sure that your uprights are well soaked and pliable. Bend down three uprights each behind the next (O). Bend these first three over your bodkin to leave a gap of about $\frac{3}{8}$ inch above the weaving for threading through at the end.

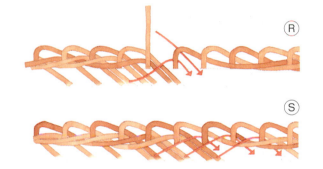

21 Take the rod on the left in front of two uprights, (one bent down and one still standing) behind the next one, and then bend the upright on the far left behind and down alongside it (P).

22 Repeat this sequence with the next weaver on the left, and then once again. From now on you will be faced with pairs of weavers (Q). The right weaver of the pair on the left (1) goes in front of two uprights (one bent down and one standing (2) and behind the next (3). The first upright (2) bends behind and down alongside (1). Continue in this way, keeping the border level with the top of the basket, and when you get back to the

beginning, thread the weaver and last remaining upright under the first stake bent down (R).

23 Thread the remaining three rods in front of two stakes and behind one stake to complete the border (S). All this can seem a bit confusing until you have done several baskets and developed an eye for it. It may help to remember that the last rods are following the same sequence as all the others in the border. Now snip off all the ends, inside and out, and stand back and admire your work.

close-up

| Base | Side weaving | Border |

hedgerow tray

For me, making this hedgerow tray turned out to be a real celebration of the range of colors and textures nature has to offer. Most of the woods were gathered on one walk down a country lane on a cold day surrounded by winter mists. Hedgerow materials have so much character of their own that I think it best not to detract from them by choosing too complicated a pattern of weaves. Therefore, this project simply uses the pairing weave.

raw materials

Prepare the following hedgerow woods according to the instructions on pages 8–12:

8 wild willow base sticks approx. 20 inches long and up to $\frac{3}{8}$ inch in diameter at base

Several lengths of hanging ivy for tying in the slath

A selection of thin rods for base and side weaving, here used: dogwood, ash, wild willow, privet, hazel, field maple and ivy

32 lime rods for the side stakes approx. 3 to 4 feet long (if you can't find lime, substitute another pliable wood such as willow or dogwood)

14 medium thickness dogwood rods for the upsett

other essentials

Pruners
Basketmaker's bodkin
Knife
Water spray
Hoop (same diameter as base of basket)
Rapping iron
Large smooth stone to use as weight

1 Make a four through four slath and tie it in with ivy (see steps 1–5, pages 22–24).

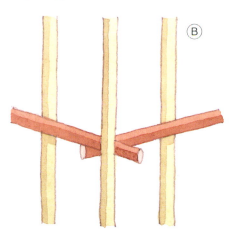

2 With the hanging ivy work in pairing weave for a few rounds while you separate out the base sticks (see steps 6–7, page 24). It is easier to do this if you work one row of weaving around pairs of base sticks first, and then singles (A).

3 Complete a few rounds of ivy, then bring in the dogwood. Continue to use pairing weave throughout. To make a join, cross the rods with the white cut ends resting on the underside of the base (B). It may be helpful to work with two sets of weavers starting opposite and chasing each other so the joins are opposite each other and the structure is balanced (A).

This little basket has a simple handle made from a length of wisteria. Slype the handle wood, push it into the border alongside a stake, and bend it into an arch. Thread it through to the inside of the basket under the border on the other side. Wind it back on itself over the handle three times. Repeat until your handle is thick enough or your length of wood runs out. Thread the end away under the border.

variation

4 Continue joining in new hedgerow rods as necessary, until the base measures about 16 inches in diameter. Spray the weavers with water to prevent them from becoming dry and brittle.

5 Slype all the lime side stakes on the belly side of the curve, and push them into the base, slyped side downwards (see step 10, page 24). Bend up the rods with extreme care. This is easier if you really push the bodkin into them where you want them to bend. Gather the stakes into a hoop.

6 Weave an upsett in dogwood (see steps 11–14, pages 25–26).

7 Now work in stripes of pairing around the sides as for the base, layering the various thin wild woods.

8 When the basket is about 4 inches deep, rap down the work well with a rapping iron, to make sure it is level. Remove the hoop if you haven't done so already.

9 Prepare to work a trac border. The most basic trac is worked by bending each side stake down in front of the next, and leaving the end resting behind the next upright along (C).

10 Alternatively, a slightly deeper, denser border can be formed. Bend down the first side stake behind one upright, in front of two then behind one, and leave it resting on the inside of the basket (D). When you bend this first rod down make sure you leave a gap just big enough for three other rods to pass underneath it. Bend the next rod down following the same sequence, and so on all the way round the basket. The snappy hedgerow side stakes will need support and encouragement

when it comes to bending over. To help them bend without snapping, prick them with the point of the basketmaker's bodkin where they leave the top row of weaving. Make sure your fingers are not in the firing line. If a stake does snap, simply slype it and push it back into the weaving.

11 When you get back to the beginning, thread the last few stakes away to complete the sequence and snip off the ends.

close-up

Siding

Trac border

woven rush baskets

When first gathered, *Scirpus lacustris*, or the common bulrush, is a lively shade of green. Rushes conjure up scenes of dragonflies, herons, swans, stillness, daydreams and lingering summer. They are great to work with because they are very soft and pliable, and the techniques for weaving them are similar to or the same as those used for willow. These rush baskets are woven over molds.

raw materials

Prepare the following rushes according to the instructions on pages 14–15:

FOR THE ROUND BASKET:

Approx. a third of a bundle of rushes sorted as follows:

14 rods 25 inches long, cut from the butt ends of the thickest rushes for the checkweave base and side stakes. These should be evenly matched in thickness.

4 thick rods for extra side stakes

16 20-inch big rods cut from the butt ends of the thickest remaining rushes for the lid

Remaining thin and medium rods for base and side weaving, these can vary in thickness (as a general rule use the thicker ones at the bottom and the thinner ones near the top)

FOR THE RECTANGULAR BASKET:

Approx. half a bundle of rushes sorted as follows:

28-inch rods cut from the butt ends of the thickest rushes for the checkweave base and side stakes, these should be evenly matched in thickness

26-inch rods cut from the butt ends of the thickest remaining rushes for the lid

Use the remaining rushes for the base and side weaving, these can vary in thickness

other essentials

Pruners

Water spray

Rush threader

Mold, round, straight-sided approx. $7\frac{1}{2}$ inches in diameter by 4 inches in height for the round basket, or rectangular, straight-sided approx. 9 x 5 x 6 inches for the rectangular basket

String

Scissors

preparation

CHOOSING A MOLD

Because rushes are soft they need to be woven over a mold in order to hold their shape. It is important that the mold has smooth sides, or it will be impossible to remove it from the finished basket. For the same

(A)

reason it must not be narrower at the top than the bottom. A block of wood (sanded smooth), a sturdy cardboard box wrapped in polyethylene or a straight-sided cake tin is ideal. Very minor ridges, such as the rim on a cake tin, can be overcome by wrapping in plenty of newspaper and parcel tape. Finally, wrap any newspaper or cardboard on your mold in polyethylene to protect it from the damp.

making the round basket

1 Before you use each rush pull it through a damp cloth to clean and flatten it and expel the air. First you need to weave a square of checkweave at the center of the base. Lay seven of the checkweave rushes in a row, alternating the butt and tip ends. Anchor them in the middle with the side of your hand. To weave in the remaining seven, lift the first, third, fifth and seventh secured rods and insert a rush. Then lift the second, fourth and sixth secure rods and insert another rush (A). Repeat these steps once, then turn the work round (this keeps the weaving central) and weave in the remaining three base rushes. Remember to alternate the butt and tip ends and get the weaving as dense and gap-free as possible.

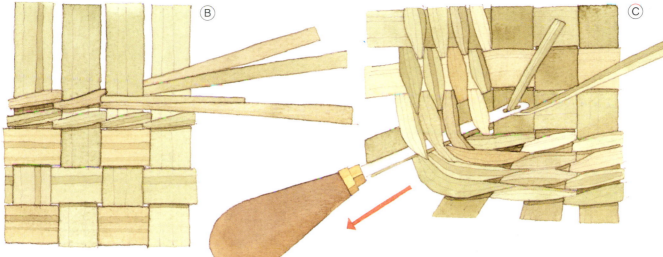

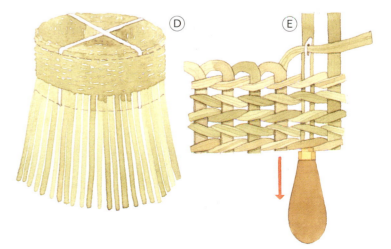

2 Work round this square of weaving using the pairing weave (steps 6–7, page 24). In rushwork, pairing is started by looping a rush weaver round one of the stakes at the end of a row. Make a loop (bend) in the weaver a third of the way down it's own length so as to stagger the ends. Continue pairing using each end of the rush as a separate weaver until one gets a bit thin or starts to run out. Join in a new weaver by looping it, just below the tip, around the stake between the two existing weavers (B). Weave the old and new ends together for a few strokes, twisting the rushes to conceal the old ends. Spray the rushes with water to prevent them from drying out.

3 Work at fanning out your corner stakes and getting them evenly spaced. Your base should become circular as it grows. When it is about 7 inches in diameter, diagonally thread in an extra side stake on each corner of the checkweave square using a rush threader (C).

4 Tie the base to your mold with string and bend the base sticks, to meet the sides of the mold and form the side stakes. Turn the work on its side and start to pairing weave up the sides of the basket (D). Weave over the string. When you cut through it to release the basket from the mold you will be able to pull it all out.

5 After the first round or so of side pairing weave you may want to loop another rush weaver round a stake and start a set of reverse pairing (see steps 4 and 9, pages 47–48). The two sets of weavers, pairing and reverse pairing, follow each other round and the resulting weave is called chain pairing. However, this is an optional step; you can just continue pairing if you wish.

6 When the work reaches the top of the mold, thread the ends of your weavers down into the side weaving and start to work a simple border. Damp your uprights if they have become dry and brittle. You can also cut points on their ends to make them easier to thread. Use the rush threader to pull each stake down alongside the next, through the top four or five rows of weaving. Stagger the number of rows through which you draw each one; the ends will blend in better if they are not all at exactly the same level (E). Cut off the ends, pulling slightly on each so that it springs back into the weaving. Leave the basket on the mold while you weave the lid.

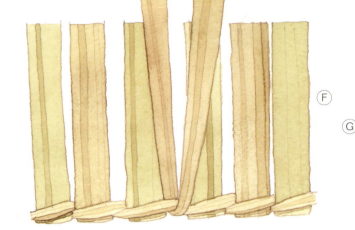

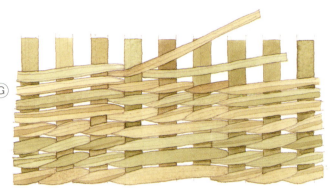

7 The lid is woven over the base of the basket to ensure a good fit. The techniques are exactly the same as for the main basket, except that the checkweave square uses eight stakes woven through eight to account for the slightly wider diameter. Border off when the weaving is about 1½ inches deep. Leave to dry on the mold overnight in an airing cupboard or somewhere warm, then remove from the mold to let air get to the inside of the basket and prevent mildew forming.

making the rectangular basket

1 The base of the rectangular basket is woven entirely in checkweave (as shown in step 1 of the round basket on page 32). Weave an area 9 x 5 inches, then tie the base to the mold. Work one row of pairing all the way round the edge of the weaving.

2 The weave used on the side, block pairing, needs a number of stakes divisible by six to work. If you haven't got the right number (as here) add in more stakes by looping a thick rush through the back of the pairing alongside an existing stake (F). Each end forms a

new stake. Do this at intervals round the basket, as many times as is necessary. You can also reduce the number of stakes by weaving two together as one.

3 Pair weave round three stakes as usual, and then round a block of three. Continue for five rounds or until the blocks look square, then switch round the order of singles and groups (G). When you have woven 4 inches of the way up the sides, continue in ordinary pairing.

4 Complete the border in the same way as for the round basket (see step 6). Make sure your stakes are well soaked for this.

5 The lid is woven over the base of the basket. Use the same technique as for the main body of the basket, starting with a checkweave base. Take care to judge the order of the block pairing weave so that the pattern continues on from the sides of the basket. Finish with a good solid round of pairing. Leave to dry on the mold overnight.

close-up

Checkweave

Chain pairing

Rectangular basket without lid

little egg **basket**

This little egg basket would also be handy for holding clothes pins, or displaying bundles of lavender. You could also fill it with buns and give it to a friend. It has a decorative handle woven from skeins of willow and hazel.

raw materials

Soak and mellow the following willow (see page 8):

UNSTRIPPED WILLOW, either *Salix purpurea* or Black Maul (both shown in photograph on page 7)

8 base sticks, approx. 1 foot long, cut from the butt ends of medium thickness rods in a 6-foot bundle

16 thin 4-foot rods for base weaving

32 medium thickness 5-foot rods for the side stakes

14 thin 5-foot rods for the upsett

4 sticks for the handle liners, taken from the butts of thick 6-foot rods

30 thin 4-foot rods for the English randing

12 thin 4-foot rods for the top wale

5 thick 6-foot or 7-foot rods for the handle bow

8 5-foot rods for splitting (see Cleaving Wood To Make Skeins, right) to bind the handle

GREEN HAZEL

A couple of silvery hazel poles for splitting (see Cleaving Wood To Make Skeins, right), approx. $\frac{1}{2}$–$\frac{2}{3}$ inches in diameter, newly gathered, with buds at the top of the branch which will be sappy and slightly pliable

other essentials

Pruners

Knife

Basketmaker's bodkin

Water spray

Hoop (approx. 1 inch larger than the diameter of the base)

Large, smooth stone to use as weight

Rapping iron

$6\frac{1}{2}$-inch panel pins and small hammer

preparation

CLEAVING WOOD TO MAKE SKEINS

Cleaving is a technique used to split willow or other woods into thin ribbons. Split woods will go twice as far as whole rods and make a more lightweight basket. You can cleave woods that are otherwise too thick to work if used whole, and you can also use skeins to bind decorative handles.

Green wood is probably the easiest to cleave. Seasoned wood is traditionally split when still dry, though I sometimes think it is easier to control when soaked. You can try either and decide for yourself which you think works best. If you do use dry wood then soak the skeins in warm water for about 3 hours or until pliable. However, you should not do this until you are sure that you are ready to work the handle.

❏ Slype your rod just below the tip, and split the slype with the knife. Take care of your fingers, keeping them behind the knife, not in the direction in which it is going (A).

❏ Put the rod under your right arm and pull the split apart with your hands, applying equal pressure on each side (B, see page 37). Carry on until you have split all along the rod's length.

Ⓐ

- If the split goes too far off to one side (C), apply more pressure to the other side. Don't worry if some of the skeins "go wrong" halfway down. Save the good sections; they will probably be long enough to use.
- Once you've split all the wood, use the knife to remove the pith that runs through the middle, so you are left with even, flat ribbons of wood. Work slowly, holding the knife steady in your right hand and drawing the skein through towards you and downwards. If you slice a skein in half, don't worry, just keep the two halves. You can use them both.

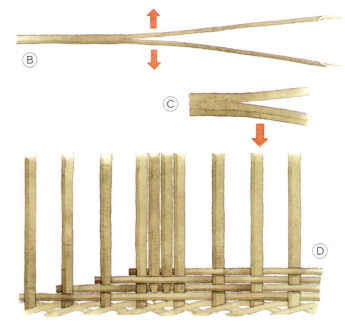

1 Weave a round base as described in steps 1–9 on pages 22–24, only this time thread four sticks through four. Your completed base should measure approximately 8 inches. Spray the wood with water so it doesn't become dry and brittle.

2 Take the side stakes and slype each one on the belly of its natural curve. Push the uprights into the base with the slyped side upwards, one on each side of every base stick. This basket has slightly curved sides so you are staking up with the curve (see step 10, page 24). Gather the side stakes into a hoop.

3 Work an upsett using a four rod wale for the first row, then drop a rod and continue with three rod waling (see steps 11–14, pages 25–26).

4 When the weaving is about 2 inches deep, stand the basket upright on a work surface with a rock or something heavy inside it to weigh it down, and rap down the weaving with a rapping iron.

5 Slype the thick handle liner rods on their tip ends. Insert two of the handle liners in between a pair of side stakes on each side of the basket (D). These rods make a space for your handle. When you have bordered off you will pull them out.

6 Prepare to work a band of English randing. This is

worked with the same number of weavers as you have spaces between the uprights, in this case 30. Find the shortest English randing weaver. Lay the butt end into any space and weave it in and out, in front of one, behind one. When you get to the handle liners, treat the four consecutive stakes as one (D). Continue the English randing weave until you get back to the beginning and leave the tip on the outside.

7 Take another English randing weaver and lay it in with the butt end one space further on from where the last one started. Weave it as before all the way round, and remember to stop one space further on from where the previous weaver stopped. Continue in the same way, starting off each new weaver one space on from the last, weaving it round and stopping when the tip is one space on from the last tip (E). You will eventually have started

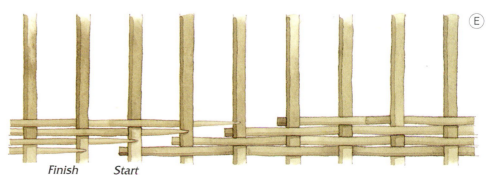

Finish   *Start*

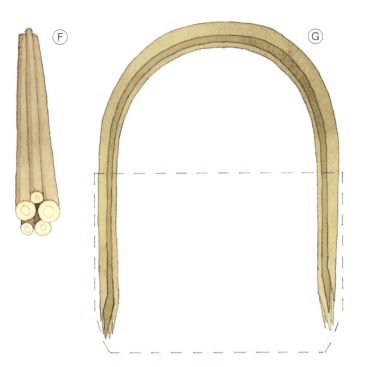

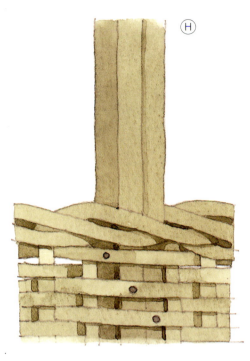

and finished one weaver in every space. The weaving will build up unevenly to start with. Don't let this phase you, it evens out again when all the weavers are in.

8 Rap down the weaving all the way round and make sure it is level. Work a band of three rod waling round the top of the basket. Remove the hoop and finish with a three rod border (see steps 20–23, pages 26–27). Pick off all the ends.

9 The decorative handle on this basket is wrapped with willow and hazel skeins. Pull out the handle liners. Group together the five thick handle bow rods, alternating the thick and thin ends. Take time to get them into an even group (F). Slype one end on the belly of each rod and push them well down into the space created by the handle liners. Bend each rod over and cut it to size, making sure the handle is in proportion to the rest of the basket. Slype the other ends and push them into the space left by the handle liners on the other side of the basket (G).

10 Nail in the handle bows. Try to get three panel pins in on either side, each going through the center of a separate handle stick and band of waling (H).

11 Take three hazel skeins that are long enough to reach right across the handle and position them next to each other. Push their ends into the basket's border in front of the handle.

12 Thread about 3 inches of the butt end of one of the willow skeins under the top rows of waling. Take it diagonally over the border and under the waling on the other side of the handle bow to form a cross (I).

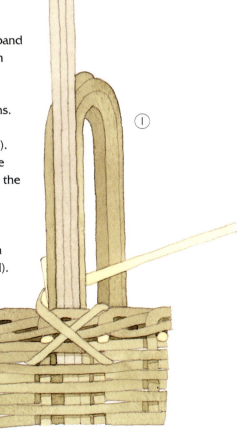

13 Bring the butt end of the willow skein up against the back of the handle and trap it there by binding around it, the handle and the hazel skeins a few times.

14 Continue to bind round the handle in the following sequence. Once under the middle hazel skein, three times under all the hazel, once under the middle hazel skein, twice over everything (J). Continue in the same way.

15 When the skein you are using is running out, lay in a new one with the bark against the underside of the handle, and bind round it for three or four turns. Then fold the old end up against the underside of the handle, and the new end takes over and binds over it (K).

16 When you have bound the whole handle, work a cross shape over the border and waling on the other side of the basket and weave the end away a few turns to secure.

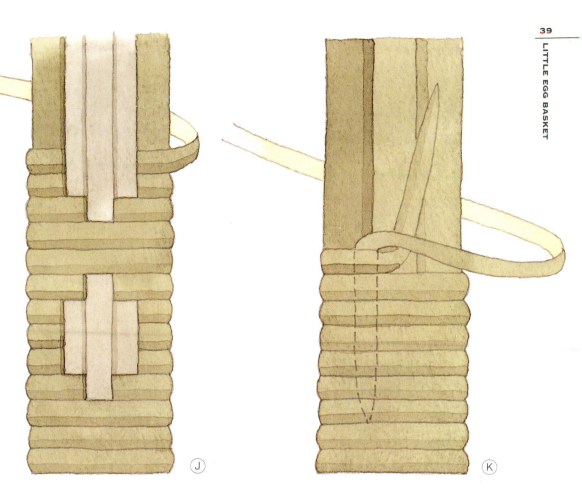

Ⓙ   Ⓚ

close-up

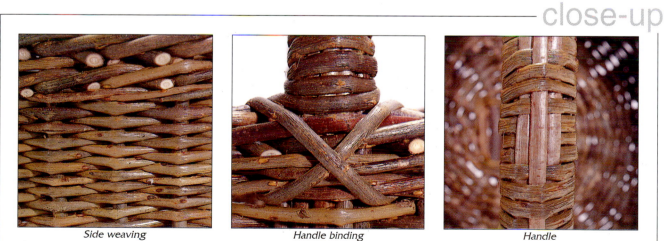

Side weaving   *Handle binding*   *Handle*

block weave
log basket

The shape of this basket and the use of block weave make it similar to the traditional bride baskets from the Schwalm region of Germany. As you will discover, block weave can be used to create striking patterns, and the resulting basket is great for holding logs.

raw materials
Soak and mellow the following willow (see page 8):

FLANDERS RED WILLOW

10 base sticks, approx. 17 inches long, cut from the butt
    ends of the thickest rods in a 7-foot bundle
4 thin 5-foot rods for base weaving
70 medium thickness 4-foot rods for side weaving

STRIPPED WHITE WILLOW

28 thin 5-foot rods for base weaving
40 medium thickness 6-foot rods for the side stakes
20 thin 6-foot rods for the upsett
70 medium thickness 4-foot rods for side weaving
12 thick 4-foot rods for the top wale
2 medium thickness 6-foot rods for the handles
2 thin 6-foot rods for the handles

other essentials
Pruners
Basketmaker's bodkin
Knife
Water spray
String
Rapping iron
Large smooth stone to use as weight

1 Make a five through five slath with the Flanders Red base sticks and tie it in with thin white willow, starting with the butts (see steps 1–5, pages 22–23).

2 Continue to pair out in white willow until the base is about $8\frac{1}{2}$ inches in diameter (see steps 6–9, page 24).

3 Now work a band of pairing using one red and one white weaver. Replace them both when they run out. Work a total of four pairs of red and white weavers. This will create a pattern of red squares. Spray the wood with water frequently to prevent it becoming dry and brittle.

4 Finish off with some more plain white pairing and stop when the diameter of the base is about $13\frac{1}{2}$ inches.

5 Stake up for a basket with straight sides using the 40 white stakes. To keep the large number of stakes under control, tie the tip ends firmly together with string rather than using the usual hoop.

6 Start your upsett with the butts of the thin white 6-foot willow. This will create a thick "foot" around the bottom of the basket. Four rod wale the first set halfway round the basket, then slype and insert a second set, also with the butts, and four rod wale them round the other half (see steps 11–13, page 25).

7 Drop a rod in each set and three rod wale them out to their tips (see steps 14–15, page 26). Keep the stakes close together and pointing upright.

8 Join in three more upsett rods on each set tip to tip, and three rod wale them out to their butts. This will be quite a sturdy row of waling which calls for you to be in an energetic mood. But it will be well worth it when you are rewarded with a really beautiful basket.

9 Rap down the weaving well. Stand the basket upright on a table or work surface with a large stone or weight inside. Join in three more upsett rods on each

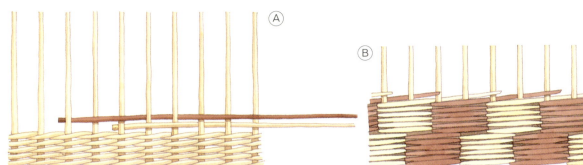

set one last time, butt to butt, and three rod wale round until you have woven about half their length. Stop before the weavers get thin, at a point when they are directly above where the very first set of waling began. Rap everything down well. Untie the stakes when they are pointing upright at the desired angle.

10 Start to block weave. This weave needs a number of stakes divisible by four (as here, 40). Take ten Flanders Red and ten white willow side weavers. Start anywhere. Take a white weaver and lay it in a space with the butt on the inside. Weave it in front of two uprights, behind two and then leave it sticking out to the front of the basket.

11 Take a red weaver. Start two spaces to the left of where the white weaver began. Lay the red weaver in, also with the butt on the inside. As with the first weaver, pass it in front of two uprights, behind two and then stop on the outside of the basket (A).

12 Repeat this sequence, moving round two spaces to the left each time and alternating the red and white weavers. When you get back to the beginning, lift up the first two weavers slightly to insert the last two. Your ten Flanders Red and ten white weavers are now all in and you will have a willow rod sticking out of every space all the way round the basket.

13 Weave in all the loose ends, starting anywhere and weaving each rod in front of two uprights, behind two and then repeating the sequence with the rod on the left. Carry on working the rods in this manner until one of them runs out. Leave the tips on the outside of the basket. In order to be effective, block weave needs beating down well with your rapping iron every round.

14 Take another set of ten red and ten white weavers and start them off in the same way as the last set, except that this time you will place the butts in the spaces that didn't get used last time (B). Start by putting a white butt above a white block.

15 The third round will also start with a white weaver laid in above a white block. The fourth and fifth rounds will start with a white weaver laid in above a red block. The sixth and seventh rounds will start with a white weaver above a white block.

16 Your basket will probably be about $9\frac{1}{2}$ inches high now (it really doesn't matter if your measurements are different). Add a few rows of three rod wale round the top of the block weaving.

17 Make sure everything is level, or as level as you want it, and work a four rod border. This is worked on the same basis as the three rod border (see steps 20–23, pages 26–27) only this time you start by bending down four rods, each behind one upright. Then take the rod on the left in front of three uprights (two bent down and one still standing) and behind one before bending the next upright (1) down (C).

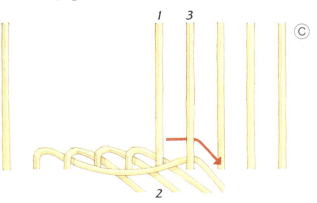

18 Continue this sequence. Upright (2) will weave next and upright (3) will bend down alongside it. Thread away the right weaver in each of the remaining pairs to complete the border (D). It should look the same all the way round. Pick off all the ends, inside and out.

(D)

19 To make twisted rod side handles, take two well soaked and mellowed white willow rods for each handle, one thicker than the other. Slype the butt end of the thicker one. Use your bodkin to make a space for it behind a stake in the border of your basket and push it in.

20 Arch the rod over into a handle shape and kink it where it will meet the border on the other side. Twist the rod up to the kink. This will require some practice. The action is a bit like cranking a handle. Hold the rod steady with your left hand about one-third of the way down, while your right hand holds it just below the tip and turns it in a circular motion (E). This will be easier if you put the basket on the floor and hold it steady by putting your foot in it. When the twist has accumulated on this portion of the rod move your left hand a bit further down, let your right hand follow it and carry on twisting. Twist all the way up to the kink. This will break the skin of the willow.

21 Slype and insert the thinner handle rod about five stakes further round. Arch the first rod over until the kink meets the rim, and thread the twisted length under the border to the right of the second handle rod (F).

(E)

(F)

22 Keeping up the twist, thread the end of the first rod under the handle to the front, and wind it round the handle three times, then to the front of the handle and in under the border on the other side (G).

23 Twist the second rod all the way down and wind it three times round the handle, under the border and back on itself again. Continue winding the rods back and forth across the handle (H) until all the gaps are filled, and thread their tips away under the border (I).

close-up

Base

Block weave

Handle

oval shopping basket

This is a really sturdy and characterful oval basket. It is made using a mixture of four different varieties of willow and shows how you can combine several different weaves to create decorative patterns and emphasize the different colors of the woods. This project illustrates how the techniques for making an oval basket differ from those used in round work.

raw materials

Prepare the following willow and hedgerow woods according to the instructions on pages 8 and 12. You can substitute any alternative variety of willow, although it is best to stick to Flanders Red, *viminalis* or *purpurea* for this type of handle as Black Maul tends to peel when twisted.

UNSTRIPPED BLACK MAUL WILLOW

7 base sticks, approx. $12\frac{3}{4}$ inches long, cut from the butt ends of thick 6-foot rods

3 base sticks, approx. 16 inches long, cut from the butt ends of thick 6-foot rods

About 24 medium thickness 4-foot rods for the chain pairing

4 thick rods, approx. $\frac{3}{8}$ inch in diameter and 1 foot long, for the handle liners

FLANDERS RED WILLOW

About 32 thin 4-foot rods for base weaving

34 thin 6-foot rods for the side stakes

14 medium thickness 5-foot rods for the upsett

24 30-inch rods taken from the butts of the thin 6-foot Flanders Red for the side wales

12 thin 4-foot rods for the top wale

4 thin 7-foot rods for the handle rope (prepare some spares, and make sure they are thoroughly soaked, mellowed and pliable)

3 medium thickness 7-foot rods for the handle bow

OTHER WOODS

About 24 medium thickness 4-foot rods of willow variety *fragilis* for the chain pair

34 thin 3-foot rods of wild willow for the English randing

other essentials

Pruners

Basketmaker's bodkin

Knife

Water spray

Hoop (1 inch larger than the base of the basket)

Rapping iron

Large smooth stone to use as weight

1 To make an oval base, use a basketmaker's bodkin to pierce the seven shorter Black Maul base sticks, and thread the three longer base sticks into the holes (see steps 1–3, pages 22–23). Arrange the seven shorter sticks about 1 inch apart, with a pair at each end.

2 Weave an oval base by pairing two sets of weavers that start at opposite corners and follow each other round (see steps 4–5 and 6–7, pages 23–24). Weave round the sticks at the ends in groups and work round the sticks along the length singly (A).

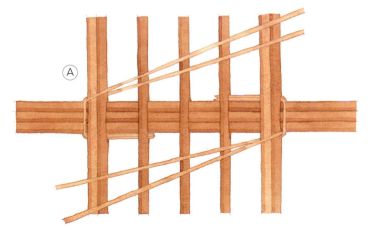

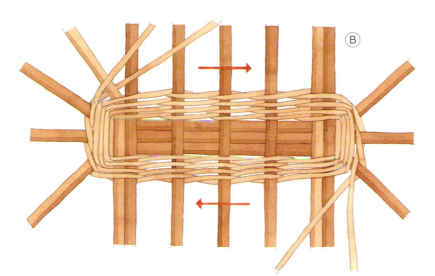

3 After the first four rounds, open out the end sticks and weave round them individually (B). Spray the wood with water to prevent it from becoming dry and brittle, and join in new weavers just before the previous ones run out (see steps 8–9, page 24).

4 Oval bases have a tendency to twist. Counteract this by switching to reverse pairing when you are halfway through. Reverse pairing is pairing (C) woven upside down. Put both your weavers to the back of the work (D). Form each stroke by bringing the weaver on the left up to the front and taking it over the other weaver, and round to the back again in the next space (E).

5 When your base measures about 14 x 9½ inches you are ready to stake up. Slype the Flanders Red side stakes on the belly of the curve, and insert them with the slyped side up so that the curve of the willow will be in harmony with the rounded shape of the basket. Insert one stake on each side of the sticks that started off in groups at the ends of the base, and just one stake alongside each of the single base sticks (F). Notice how the single stakes all go in to the left of each stick on one side of the base and to the right on the other.

6 Bend and gather the stakes into a hoop and weave an upsett in Flanders Red willow (see steps 11–14, pages 25–26).

7 Stand the basket upright on a work surface, and put a weight inside it. Take three of the side wale Flanders Red rods. Starting with their tip ends, work a three rod wale halfway round the basket, from the middle of one side to the middle of the other (see step 14, page 26). Join in three more Flanders Red rods, this time with butts,

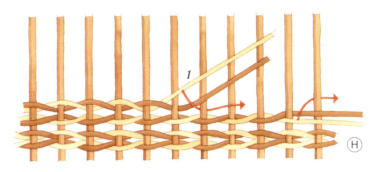

and wale back round to the start (G). Thread the ends away to complete the round. Because the weavers are quite thick you will need to really support each stake with your left hand as you weave round it, so that they don't distort the shape of your basket. All this hard work will pay you back in the form of a beautifully individual basket.

8 Rap down the weaving frequently to make sure it is dense, measuring as you go to check that the height of each band of weaving is level.

9 Begin chain pairing. This weave is created by pairing two weavers. When they have gone halfway round, insert a second pair of weavers working reverse pairing. The two sets follow each other round. If you find it awkward working with the weavers on the inside of the basket you can reverse pair with the weavers on the outside of the basket, taking the one on the left (1) underneath the one on the right (H). Each pair consists of one Black Maul and one *fragilis* weaver. Make sure that you put the second set in the right way to create the vertical stripes of color.

10 Rap down the weaving and work a row of three rod wale in Flanders Red. Start the thin ends off on the opposite side to where they started last time you worked this weave.

11 Rap everything down again, and work a section of English randing (see steps 6–7, page 37) using wild willow. This weave is worked with the same number of weavers as you have spaces between uprights, in this case 34. Note that unlike the egg basket, the handle liners are not inserted into this basket until after the English randing. This is because it is a deeper basket with more bands of dense weaving to follow and if you insert them at this stage, they may prove hard to remove later on.

12 Slype the thin ends of the thick willow to make handle liners. Insert the slyped end of two of these

to the left of the central stakes on each side of the basket. They are to make a space for your handle and will be removed later. Work another band of Flanders Red three rod wale.

13 Rap down well and do as much chain pairing as is necessary to bring the overall height of the basket to about $8\frac{1}{2}$ inches.

14 Weave a fourth band of three rod wale in Flanders Red. Rap everything down well, and, using the thinnest Flanders Red weavers, do a shallow band of three rod waling. Rap down the weaving and check it is level. Remove your hoop if you haven't done so already.

15 Insert two more pieces of slyped willow alongside each of the handle liners to be really sure that there will be plenty of room to insert a thick handle.

16 Work a thick five rod behind two border. A tip here is to start the border where the handle will be inserted, as the start/finish point of the border is usually slightly untidy and the handle will detract from this. The underlying principle of this is the same as for a three rod border (see steps 20–23, pages 26–27), only this time start by bending down five rods, each behind two uprights. Remember to leave a gap big enough for threading away at the end.

17 Take the weaver on the left, bring it in front of four stakes (two of these are bent down and two are still standing), behind one and bend the next upright down alongside it (I). Continue around the border repeating this sequence. When

you encounter pairs of weavers use the right weaver of the left pair. The other one is finished. When you have worked your way back around to the beginning, thread away the ends to complete the border. Pick off the ends inside and outside your basket.

18 Pull out the handle liners. Make a thick handle bow from three 7-foot Black Maul rods, slyped and inserted in the spaces created by the handle liners.

19 Slype and insert four thin 7-foot Flanders Red rods, two on each end of the handle, immediately to the left of the bow. Twist the rod nearest to the inside of the basket (see step 20, page 43). Wind it five times around the handle, then thread it under the border to the inside of the basket. Bring it up and wind it back around the handle in between the first windings.

20 Secure the end temporarily in the side weaving of the basket. Turn the basket round and work the equivalent rod on the other side in the same way (J).

21 Now twist the remaining two rods and wind each round the handle immediately under its neighbour. Thread each one under the border and wind it

back across the handle to where it started. Thread the tips away under the handle rope and under the border.

22 If a piece of bark peels off your handle to make a bold white patch just where you really don't want it, you can stick it back in place with wood glue. Don't fuss over it too much though; you're weaving with plants that are wild and natural and there is a case to be made for them being most beautiful as they come, blemishes and all.

close-up

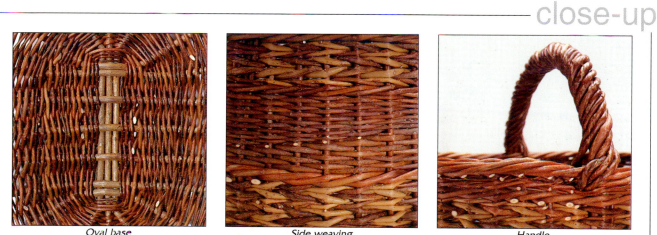

Oval base   Side weaving   Handle

frame baskets

the framework of this style of basket is made from a hoop or hoops into which ribs are inserted. This technique determines the overall shape of the finished piece, whether a flat oval like the cake racks (see below), or more similar to a boat shape (see Willow Skein Frame, Basket, pages 54–57). Thinner strands can then be woven around the basic skeleton to fill it in.

hoop frame
cake rack

If you, as I do, enjoy making cakes and buns for your friends and family, then they'll be even more charmed when you serve them from a homemade cake cooling rack. This project introduces plenty of new techniques – bending a frame, openwork, carving a scallom and fitching – and yet they're not too difficult. Happy making and baking.

raw materials
Soak and mellow the following willow (see page 8):

STRIPPED WHITE WILLOW

1 stick, approx. 5 feet long, cut from the butt end of the thickest rods in a 8-foot bundle, for the frame (plus a couple of spares to practise with)

About 4 5-foot skeins (see Cleaving Wood To Make Skeins, page 35)

About 22 evenly matched thin 6-foot rods for the ribs

About 4 medium thin 4-foot rods for the fitching

other essentials
Pruners
Knife
Pencil
Water spray
Basketmaker's bodkin

1 To make the frame, first take the thickest rod. Make a long (approx. $8\frac{1}{2}$ inches) very gradual slype on the inside of the butt end and a slightly shorter, shallow slype on the outside of the tip end. Ease the rod round into an oval hoop. The butt end will need more encouragement to bend than the tip. Support the middle of the willow against your stomach as you draw the ends together. The ends should overlap by about 10 inches.

2 To bind the overlap securely, trap the butt end of a skein between the slyped ends of your hoop. Wind it round the hoop along to one end of the slype then back to the other end (A). To finish, wind the skein back to the middle. Secure the end by threading it under the previous binding for a few turns.

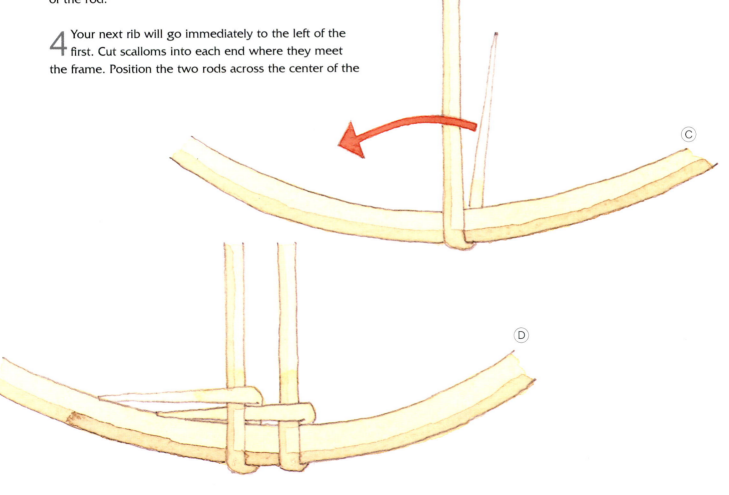

Ⓑ

3 Now prepare the scalloms. A scallom is a scooped tongue cut at the end of a rod. Take the thin willow rods for the ribs and cut them into smaller rods, from the butt ends, that are about 1 foot longer than the width along the length of the frame. Take one of these smaller rods and hold it against the hoop slightly to the left of center. It should have equal lengths protruding from either side of the frame. Mark on the rod with a pencil the points at which it touches the hoop at each end. These are the points at which you will need to make the scoops (B). Keep your fingers out of the path of the knife and cut away from you making a scoop long enough to bend round the rim of the hoop followed by a tail about 3½ inches long. Repeat on the other end of the rod.

4 Your next rib will go immediately to the left of the first. Cut scalloms into each end where they meet the frame. Position the two rods across the center of the hoop, alternating the thick and thin ends to keep everything well balanced.

5 Bend the scoop of the scallom of the first rod you prepared over and around the frame. Bring the tail up from under the frame on the right-hand side of the rib. Take it leftwards over the top of the rib and down towards the back of the work (C). The tails on this side of the center will all point towards the left. Spray the wood with water to prevent it from becoming dry.

6 Tie the next rod on in the same way. Every time you tie in a new scallom, incorporate the tails of the previous sticks into your binding (D).

Ⓒ

Ⓓ

7 Continue until you have attached all the rods to the left-hand edge of the frame, keeping them as close together as possible. Now attach the rods on the right-hand side of the frame. The tails of these scalloms will all point to the right. Leave the scalloms at the top of the hoop untied for now.

8 Start to add the two rows of fitching, evenly spaced apart, across the ribs. This weave is specifically for openwork baskets. It is quite similar to pairing but the twist is in the opposite direction, and the willows really grip the stakes holding them much more firmly in place. Take two evenly matched medium thin fitching rods and bend them smoothly round a basketmaker's bodkin about one-third of the way down from their tips. Loop these two rods around the frame as if they were one strand (E).

9 Make a half twist downwards with the rods and take one pair over and one pair under the first stick. Half twist to grip it in place, then work the pairs around the next rib as before (F).

10 Continue until you reach the other end. Take the weavers around the frame and fitch weave them back again, about halfway across. Leave the ends on the back of the work.

11 Complete the second row of fitching in the same way, but start on the opposite side of the hoop from where the first row began.

12 Tie your still-loose scalloms to the hoop at the end. They will probably be bone dry by now, so give them a good soak first.

willow skein
frame basket

Frame baskets truly belong to the countryside and probably originated in Europe, where people such as gypsies, farmers and fishermen made them for use at work and in the home. This project uses "green" – newly gathered – willow, variety *viminalis*, because it produces some of the stoutest rods for a thick handle and rim. If you can't find any *viminalis* you could substitute hedgerow willow or any other newly gathered willow that is thick enough. You could make this project entirely from green willow, but using seasoned (dry) ribs and bindings will help to guard against it becoming rickety due to shrinkage.

raw materials

GREEN WILLOW

For information on gathering and preparing green woods, see Preparing Hedgerow Woods, page 12. For this project use unstripped green willow. It is much easier to bend into hoops in this state, than when it has been dried and re-soaked.

2 thick, tall rods, up to approx. $\frac{2}{3}$ inches diameter (you could gather up to ten rods so that you can have a few trial runs), for the frame and handle hoops

At least 50 stout 7- to 8-foot rods for splitting (see Cleaving Wood To Make Skeins, page 35) for the weaving

DRY WILLOW

Soak and mellow the following unstripped dry willow (see page 8). I used *viminalis* but use Black Maul if you don't have any *viminalis* that is seasoned.

2 5-foot skeins (see Cleaving Wood To Make Skeins, page 35) to bind the hoops

At least 4 thin 5-foot rods for the bindings

16 medium thickness 6-foot rods for the ribs

other essentials

Pruners
Knife
Parcel tape
String
$\frac{5}{8}$-inch panel pins and small hammer
Water spray

preparation

3 WEEKS IN ADVANCE

☐ Make the handle and frame hoops. Form the two thickest green willow rods into two hoops, a round one (the handle hoop) about $12\frac{3}{4}$ inches in diameter, and an oval one (the rim hoop) about $11\frac{1}{2}$ inches wide and 21 inches long, as described in Step 1, page 51. Make sure the slyped ends overlap by at least 10 inches. Bind the joins securely at each end with parcel tape instead of willow skein.

☐ Make sure the frame hoop will fit inside the handle hoop. Tie some string around the middle of the oval hoop to keep it in shape and stop it reverting to a circle. Bring the hoops inside and let them dry to shape in a warm place, ideally in an airing cupboard, for about three weeks.

1 WEEK IN ADVANCE

☐ Soak the willow for the ribs and bindings

☐ Cleave the green willow rods for weaving (see page 35) and keep them in a sheltered area outside where they won't dry out.

1 To prepare the frame, undo the tape and bind the hoops with willow skein. Where the wood is thick enough, tap a panel pin through each join. Take care that the point of the pin does not protrude out the other side. Put the rim hoop inside the handle hoop. Make sure the hoops are central and secure with a panel pin where they meet on each side (A).

2 Select a piece of whole, slender willow and use it to bind the rim hoop to the handle. Make sure you have the basket the right way up, with the join in the handle

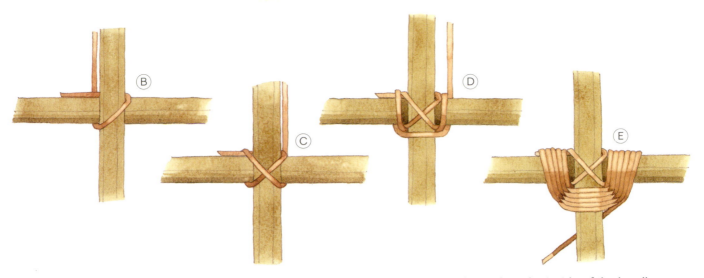

hoop at the bottom. Put the tip of the binding rod horizontally behind the handle hoop. Bind it round the handle and rim to form a cross shape (B–C).

3 Weave down in front of the horizontal rod, across and behind the vertical, up and in front of the next horizontal, back down and behind that same horizontal, across and in front of the vertical and up and behind the first horizontal to take you back to where you started (D). Spray the wood with water so it doesn't dry out.

4 Continue weaving in the same way until the weaver runs out. Rest the end of the weaver on the inside of the handle hoop (E). Join in a new thin willow rod by also resting the butt on the inside of the handle hoop, so that it crosses over the old end (F). Continue weaving the binding until you are nearly out to the tip of that weaver. Rest it on the inside of the handle hoop. Do the same on the other side of the basket where the handle and frame meet.

5 You have now made some pockets to hold the ribs of the basket. The first four ribs are marked (1) on diagram H. Slype the first end of the rib, insert it into a pocket, bend it around, cut it to size and insert the other end. The length of the first four ribs should be proportionate to the handle and rim hoops they are next to. Alternate the tip and butt ends of the willow rods.

6 Turn the basket upside down and work with the handle between your knees. To start weaving with a green

willow skein rest the end on the inside of the handle hoop (where the tip of the previous rod finished). Take it in and out of each of the ribs individually and twice over the top of the rim from now on. At this stage you will find you need to half turn the skein to keep the bark on the outside of the basket. Use the thinner skeins first, and keep the thicker, longer ones for the base, which will get more wear. Always keep the weaving on a frame basket symmetrical. Whatever you do on one side, mirror it on the other.

7 To make a join in the weaving, overlap the skeins for a couple of strokes (G). Keep the ends of joins on the inside of the basket and don't make a join on the rim or the first rib down from the rim.

8 As the circumference of the weaving grows, the space between the ribs will increase, so insert four more ribs on the inside of and into the same pocket as the first four as soon as there is room. Resume weaving and insert four more ribs as soon as possible. Continue to weave. Add the last four ribs in. This will make a total of

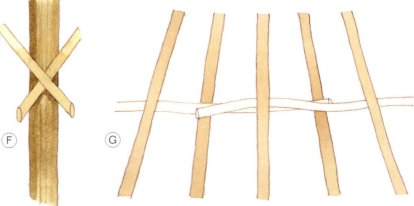

eight ribs on each side (H). The wood on the inside of the skeins tends to crack. This is part of the rustic nature of it. If they are splintering excessively try shaving them a bit thinner. Feed them in and out carefully, pushing the tip through first, supporting them, and tending to have the bark side outwards when they loop and curve. You may find it easier to modify your first basket by having just six ribs on each side so there is more space in which to weave.

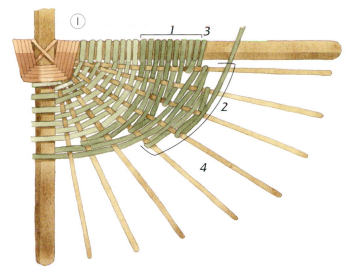

9 Work at shaping and spacing the ribs evenly. You will find that the gap yet to be woven, in the center of the basket, becomes uneven unless you do some packing – building up areas of weaving by working backwards and forwards over certain groups of ribs (I). The number of ribs you work over will decrease each time you turn a corner. Typically, packing needs to be done at each end of both sides of your basket, in the areas marked (1) and (2) on the diagram. Make sure you do a straight row of weaving (3) between each block of packing. The number of ribs to be worked over and the extent to which the weaving needs building up will vary according to how long your ribs are and the width of your skeins. Judge it so that you are left with a straight parallel gap (4) to weave your skeins into. It might occasionally be necessary to take the weaving just once round the rim, if it starts to fill up too rapidly. Weave in as many skeins as is necessary to complete the basket, and pick off the ends.

close-up

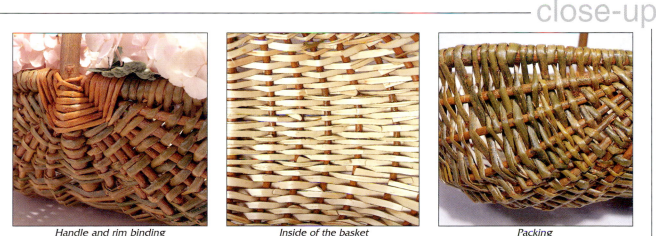

Handle and rim binding   *Inside of the basket*   *Packing*

plaiting is a basketmaking technique that takes strands, usually of equal weight and dominance, and folds and weaves them under and over each other with no definition between stake and strand. Plaiting is a natural choice for flat materials such as bands of bamboo, palm leaves and strips of birch bark, which are woven into baskets in Finland.

plaited rush
floor-mats

Rushes, grasses and garden leaves can all be plaited and the techniques used in this project produce some delightful results. Rushes have long been used as a floor covering to bring warmth to people's homes. Even in Saxon times they were spread over the cold stone and earth floors of houses and churches. As these rustic carpets were only changed a few times a year at most, the gentry used to mix in a few herbs to mask the smell. Happily rush mats are also very contemporary and look good in almost any environment.

raw materials
Prepare the following rushes according to the instructions on page 14:

$1\frac{1}{2}$ bundles of rushes of mixed thickness and length (pull each rush through a damp cloth to clean it, flatten it and expel the air before working)

other essentials
Scissors
String
Strong linen thread or twine in a natural color that will blend with rushes; rug wrap is ideal
Strong, long, large-eyed needle
Pliers
Latex gloves

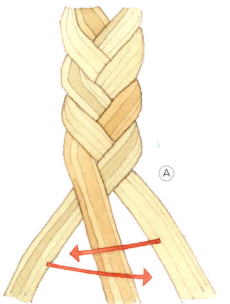

1 Form about 18 of the rushes into a bundle and tie them together at one end. Make sure they are of assorted lengths since you don't want them all to run out at the same time – some of the rushes could be bent in half to make two shorter strands. Fasten the bundle to a beam, banister or hook on the wall, then divide the bundle into three further groups. Start an ordinary three strand plait (A). Weave the groups of

(B)

(E)

A seven strand plait is flat and wide and can be used to make appealing floor-mats.

Start plaiting in the same way as the three strand plait. Once you have got this plait underway, subdivide your bundles into seven. Gradually add in a few more rushes to maintain even bundles – on average about four or five in each strand. Start to plait, bringing each outside strand over and under its three neighbours, and into the middle (E).

Three and seven strand plaits can also be sewn together to make baskets. This example uses a fine three strand plait. Coil the base and first few rounds of siding as for the center of the oval mat (see step 8, page 65 for advice on building up the sides of a coiled basket). Alternatively, make a checkweave base and use the ends of the base sticks to start the plaits. For a neat finish, thread the ends of a section of plait down into the row below with a rush threader. Continue stitching round, building the coil up, and making all sorts of patterns.

variations

rushes as one strand. Slightly twist the plait as you work to make a neat outside edge.

2 Maintain the thickness of the strands in your plait by adding in another rush whenever necessary. The thickness of the plait is more important than the actual number of rushes in each strand. Always join in with the butt. Plait all of the rushes.

3 To start sewing the mat, cut a neat end to your plait and tie some linen thread – doubled over for extra strength – around it tightly just below the end.

4 Thread the strong, long needle with the strong linen thread and make some stitches over the end of the plait to ensure it is neat and secure.

5 Start to coil the plait into an oval mat by bending it about 10 inches from the end. Sew through the middle of this double thickness plait, using ordinary running stitch. When you have stitched to the end, turn the corner and carry on coiling, bit by bit, sewing more and more of the plait to the previous round (B). Angle the needle slightly to get it through the thick plaits, and use a pair of pliers to help pull and push it. Latex gloves will help you grip the needle. Aim to hide the stitching from sight, between the coils.

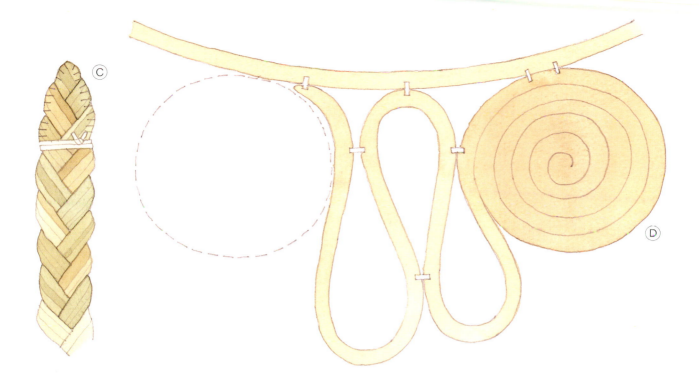

6 When your oval is about 20 x 11½ inches, finish it off by threading the ends of the rushes into the plait on the previous round.

7 Use the remaining plait to stitch the scrolls. Starting in the center of each scroll, coil the plait into tight circles, using running stitch to bind them securely. Continue until the coils are about 4¾ inches in diameter.

8 Leave enough spare plait to make two loops and then cut the plait. Cut a slight angle on the underneath of the end of the plait to make it blend in inconspicuously when you sew it to the main mat. Stitch over it and bind securely (C). Make about eight

coils and loops. Judge the spacing of the loops carefully to make sure they will all fit.

9 Sew the coils, equally spaced, very firmly round the edge of the mat. Form the loops between the coils, sewing them securely where they meet with the coils and the edge of the mat (D).

10 Sew the tops of the loops to each other only after you have sewn the bottom of the loops to the main mat, otherwise the tension will be wrong.

close-up

Loops and scrolls pattern   *Three-strand plait*   *Seven-strand plait mat*

this technique is the basketry equivalent of coiled pots, in which a central core spirals round to build up a vessel that is held together by stitches. The stitches can be spaced out and carried out in thread, so that the coiled core shows through, or the core can be completely bound over, for instance with long broad leaves.

lavender & sweet
grass basket

This coiled basket has an exposed core. I particularly like this method of basketmaking as it is comparatively easy to do using just a few basic stitches and yet it has huge creative possibilities – stunning and beautiful results are possible using just your imagination and whatever materials you can find. This project uses a simple spiral stitch to make a wonderfully colored and scented lavender basket with a sweet grass border.

raw materials
Prepare the following according to the instructions on page 13–14:

DRIED LAVENDER
9 oz with the leaves removed, divided into six
    bundles, mixed in length. Soak two bundles
    to start with and more as and when you need
    them (the flowers fall apart if they are kept damp
    for too long).

other essentials
Strong, unbleached linen thread, not too fine or it will
    cut into the materials
Heavy-duty scissors
Large-eyed needle
Grass for the rim (optional), such as a generous
    handful of dried sweet vernal grass. Gather this
    when the seedheads are still quite young or they
    will shed.

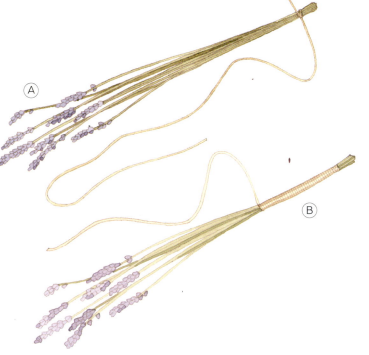

1 Take about 10 stems of lavender and tie the ends firmly together with a long piece of linen thread (A).

2 Trap the short end of the thread in the bundle, and bind tightly round for about 2 inches. Work with the lavender flowers on your left, bringing the thread from behind, over the top of the stems (B).

3 Cut away the ends of the lavender, quite close to the start of the binding, and bend the bound end into a close circle.

4 Thread the linen onto a large-eyed needle (C) and start to spiral stitch around the coil. Keeping the bundle of lavender flowers on your left, bring the thread over the top of the stems and push your needle right through the top third of the previous round. Work stitches that attach the outside coil to the inner coil, sewing into the binding. Try and get about 24 stitches into this first round. They will be quite close together and should be evenly spaced.

5 After the first round, keep coiling the lavender and make one new stitch into each of the stitches on the previous row (D and E). Keep the thickness of your core even by regularly adding in a few new stems. Blend the ends neatly into the middle of your bundle.

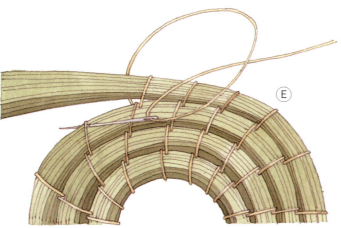

6 When your thread has almost run out, knot in a new length. Lie the knot on the outside of the coil so that the next round of lavender will cover it. Trap the old end of the thread under the next one or two stitches (F).

7 Continue coiling and stitching. Don't worry if some of the lavender flowers brush off as you work, plenty will remain. When the base measures about 6 inches in diameter, you will need to increase the number of stitches to prevent the work from becoming weak. Do this by making two stitches into each previous stitch, for one round only (G).

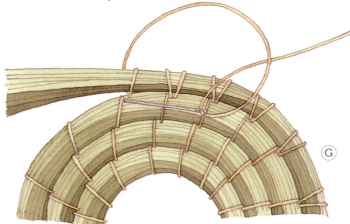

You can do a lot with spiral stitch simply by varying the materials you use, and the density of the stitching.

These baskets are made from ginger lily and unbleached linen thread, using the same technique as the lavender basket. One is decorated with its own dried seedheads (below), and the other with Eucalyptus citradora leaves (right). The ginger lily has a slightly gingery scent and the eucalyptus leaves smell faintly lemony, so these baskets have scented as well as visual appeal.

8 When the base measures about $6\frac{3}{4}$ inches in diameter, start working the sides. Turn the coil over and work with the outside of the basket facing you. Gradually steer the coil so that it starts to build up on top of the base. Try to keep the flowerheads on the outside of the bundle where you can see them, and conceal the stem ends on the inside. Hold each new coil in a position that will make the sides flow outwards.

9 When you get to the final round – my basket was about 4 inches high – fade out the coils by ceasing to add in any new stems. Continue stitching until the bundle runs out.

10 To make a decorative grass rim, stitch bundles of grass seedheads with stems about $1\frac{1}{2}$ inches long round the rim of the basket. Add in new bundles at regular intervals. The grass topping wants to be generous, it will look shabby if it's too sparse. Bring the thread over the grass with care and ensure everything sits nicely, with the new stems hidden underneath the fluffy seedheads.

wrapped coil
table-mats

This project is based on lazy squaw stitch, the name deriving from the long history of American Indian coiled basketry and is a good introduction to wrapped coiled work. Many different patterns can be created just by varying the number of wraps between each stitch. The main project (top right in picture opposite) is wrapped with montbretia leaves, but sedge, day lily and raffia would also make excellent wrapping materials, bound around a core of random mixed grasses.

raw materials

Prepare the following grasses and leaves according to the instructions on page 13):

2 generous handfuls of mixed meadow or garden grasses for the coil. These should be of varying lengths, but at least 1 foot long.

2 generous handfuls of montbretia leaves

other essentials

Large-eyed needle

Scissors

1 Take a pencil-thick bundle of grasses of mixed length. You can use them with the seedheads still on, or just use the stems if you find it easier.

2 Wrap a relatively long piece of wrapping material around the grass bundle for about $2\frac{1}{2}$–$2\frac{3}{4}$ inches, trapping the end as you wrap (A).

3 Bend the wrapped section round into a very close circle. The exposed core material should be on your left while the wrapping material comes from behind the grasses (B).

4 Thread the end of the wrapping material onto a large-eyed needle and start to work lazy squaw stitch as you continue to build up the coil. This stitch consists of alternate long and short stitches. The long stitch should wrap around two rounds of coiled material and the short stitch wraps just the core materials you are currently coiling (C). In the first round the long stitches

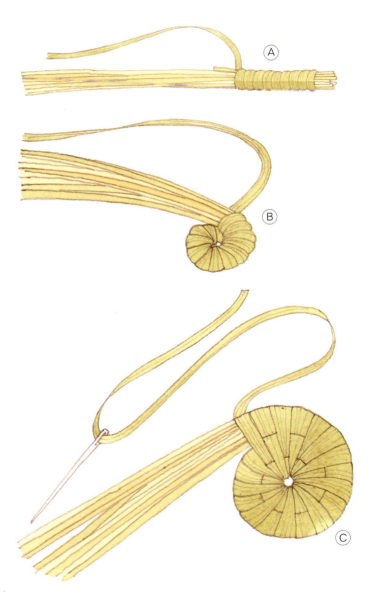

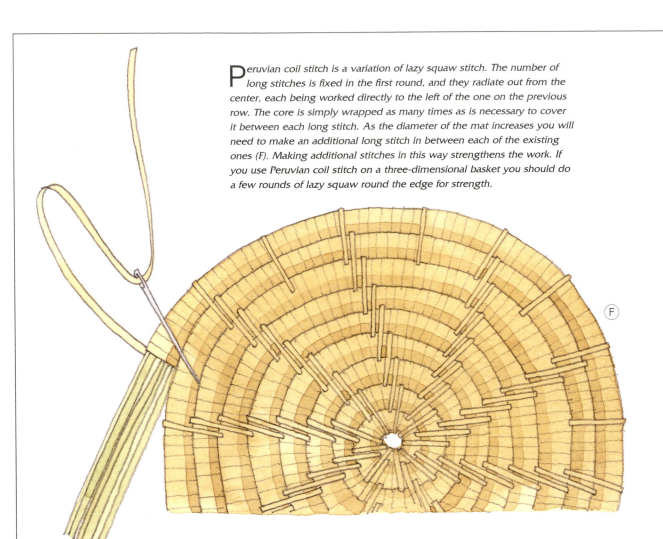

Peruvian coil stitch is a variation of lazy squaw stitch. The number of long stitches is fixed in the first round, and they radiate out from the center, each being worked directly to the left of the one on the previous row. The core is simply wrapped as many times as is necessary to cover it between each long stitch. As the diameter of the mat increases you will need to make an additional long stitch in between each of the existing ones (F). Making additional stitches in this way strengthens the work. If you use Peruvian coil stitch on a three-dimensional basket you should do a few rounds of lazy squaw round the edge for strength.

(F)

(G)

To make an oval mat, bind the core for a few turns, a short distance from the end. Bend the core where the binding ends. Use a figure-of-eight motion to wrap back along the length of the core (G). Fold the still exposed core material back to meet the wrapped core to begin coiling an oval shape. Bind the core enough times to cover it while it turns the corner, then continue coiling, working lazy squaw or Peruvian coil stitch.

The day lily oval mat has a core a bit thinner than a pencil. Start by bending the core over $4\frac{1}{2}$ inches from the end. Form eight long stitches in the first round, three along each side and one at each end. Repeat for the second and third rounds. On the fourth round, start to make the diamond shapes by increasing the number of long stitches above each long stitch on the previous round, so that there is one on either side. Every round, make one additional stitch in each group until you have groups of five in a row. From now on decrease a stitch in each group every time you make a circuit, until you have just one.

variations

will go into the center of the circle. Pull each stitch firmly round the core so the work won't become loose when it dries out. If at any point the wrapping material seems to have a weakness, or is marked, work the stitch twice for strength. Occasionally blend some more grass into your core to keep the thickness even.

5 When a piece of wrapping material is within about $2\frac{1}{2}$ inches of running out, join in by holding the base of a new piece against the core and wrapping over it a few times until it is held in place (D). This new wrapping material will now take over, binding the old end along with the core. This join should happen on a single wrap rather than a long stitch.

6 Increase as often as necessary to keep the core covered by making two long stitches into one single wrap on the previous round (E).

7 When your mat is the required size, here 8 inches in diameter, finish it off by fading out the core material over the last round. This is done by not adding any more in, and by cutting it away as necessary.

8 Thread the end of the wrapping material away by pulling it securely through the coiling on the previous round.

close-up

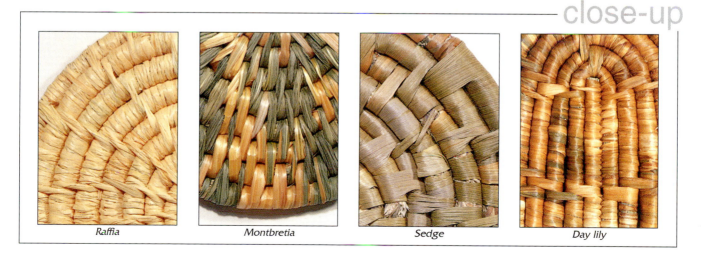

| Raffia | Montbretia | Sedge | Day lily |

berry
basket

This little coiled basket is just the thing to carry while picking wild or garden fruits. It is made from day lily leaves wrapped over a cane coiled core and is based on lazy squaw stitch.

raw materials

Prepare the following straw, leaves and center cane according to the instructions on pages 12–15:

A generous handful of straw for the base

A generous handful of day lily leaves for wrapping material

About 30 feet of ³⁄₁₆ inch diameter center cane to continue the core coil and handle

other essentials

Large-eyed needle

Knife

Round-nosed pliers

Scissors

1 Start the round base by coiling the straw and wrapping it with day lily leaves using the lazy squaw stitch (see steps 1–6, pages 67–69).

2 When the base is about $4\frac{3}{4}$ inches in diameter begin to coil the sides of the basket (see step 8, page 65).

This basket has straight sides. Make a long slype on the end of the core center cane and incorporate it into the straw core. Fade out the straw and continue to coil and wrap the cane. Make long slypes on both ends of the cane rods to make them easier to join in as you work (A).

3 Work one side row in lazy squaw stitch before you start to make the pattern of squares. Work four single wraps, followed by four lazy squaw stitches in the usual way (B). You may have to work more or less lazy squaw stitches on the last couple of blocks to make the pattern fit in.

4 Complete two more rounds, each copying the row below. On the fourth round work long stitches over all three rows of the wrapped squares (C).

5 Complete several rounds of lazy squaw stitch. For the first round after the pattern you will have to wrap the core above the squares as there will be nowhere to put the long stitches.

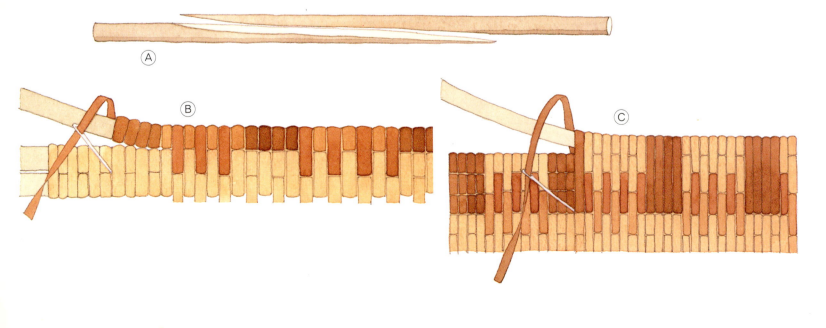

A

B

C

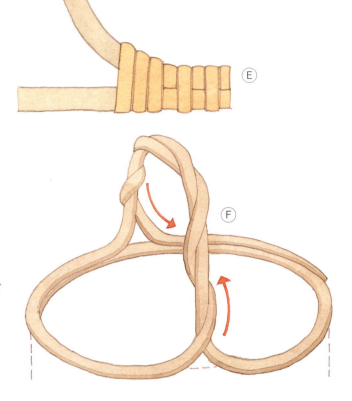

6 Repeat the pattern, this time working squares above the previous rows of lazy squaw stitch and vice versa.

7 Work two more rows of lazy squaw stitch and start to join in a piece of cane that is long enough to use as a handle. Soak this piece of cane in warm water for about 30 minutes so it is pliable enough to work with.

8 Carry the handle across the basket (D), squeezing it with round-nosed pliers to encourage it to bend where it meets the rim on each side. Wrap it as you go, and work extra long stitches at the points where it leaves the rim, as they will take the most strain (E).

9 Take the cane round the rim on the other side of the basket, until it meets the handle again. Wrap the cane and carefully wind the bound length three times round the handle, feeding the end of the rod through first and supporting it as you go (F). Carefully make a long slype on the end of the core, then fade it out and secure the end by sewing it into the previous round.

close-up

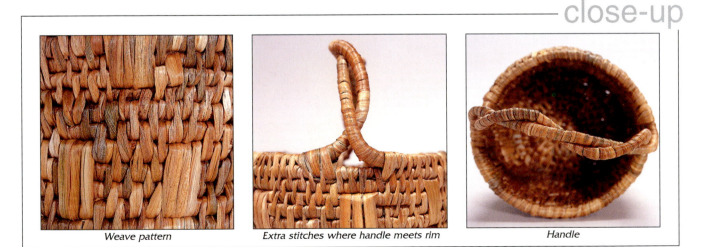

Weave pattern   *Extra stitches where handle meets rim*   *Handle*

coiled rag basket

This basket is made using strips of mixed recycled textiles bound over a cane core, resulting in a basket full of woolly charm. Select a lively bundle of fabrics. There are just two things to watch out for: the fabric should not be likely to fall apart – so knitwear should be well felted – and you will need to be able to persuade it, when cut up into narrow strips, to go through the eye of a large-eyed needle.

raw materials

8 oz of No. 6 center cane for the core
(soak a bundle of 6 of these canes following the
instructions on page 12)
Selection of washed fabrics for wrapping material

other essentials

Knife
Scissors
Round-nosed pliers
Large-eyed needle
Latex gloves
Pliers
Smaller needle suitable for sewing with linen thread
Strong linen or cotton thread
Green felt
Fabric stiffener

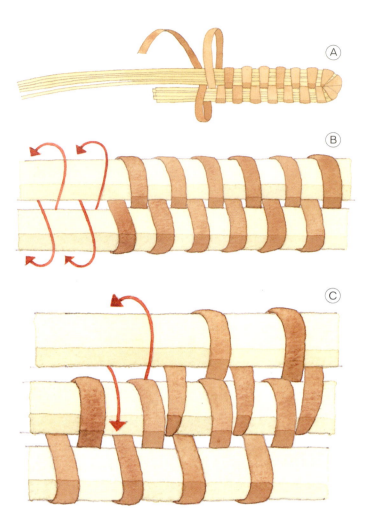

1 Cut the fabric into strips about $\frac{1}{2}$ inch wide, a bit wider
for fine fabrics, narrower for heavy, thick ones. Discard
seams and hems.

2 The core of this basket is made up of a bundle of
6 canes. Start the base by bending the cane stakes
about $2\frac{1}{2}$ inches from the end. Squash the cane where
you want it to bend with some round-nosed pliers.

3 Take a strip of rag and bind the start of the core
using navajo stitch (A). This stitch is worked by
binding the new core to the previous row in a figure-of-
eight sequence (B). Thread the wrapping material over
the top of the new core, from front to back. Next bring
it back to the front underneath the new core. Take the
fabric to the back again under the core on the previous
row and finally, thread it back to the front again in
between the new core and the previous row. Keep
repeating this sequence and note how, as the rounds
build up, the core bundle gets wrapped twice (C).

4 Work enough stitches into each round to cover the
core and keep the structure strong. You can work
two stitches into one space or miss a space if necessary.

5 Coil an oval base. You will need to work some extra
wraps around the corners to cover the core. When
your fabric strip is nearing its end, join in a new one (see

step 5, page 69). Maintain a core of six strands by
adding in new canes as necessary. Slype the ends of
these so they blend in easily.

6 Coil a base about 6 x $7\frac{1}{2}$ inches, then start working up
the sides (see step 8, page 65). Try to find a path for
the needle in between the previous stitches, rather than
plunging it straight through the fabric. You may find latex
gloves useful to help grip the needle and pliers can help
to pull it through.

7 When the basket is about $4\frac{3}{4}$ inches high, start to
make a handle. Soak the exposed cane bundle in hot
water for about 10 minutes (avoid getting the fabric wet
in case the colors run). Arch the core to form a handle
and use round-nosed pliers to bend it where it meets the
rim of the basket on either side. Bind the core round the
rim (leaving the handle exposed), fading it out gradually
by cutting away the canes one by one.

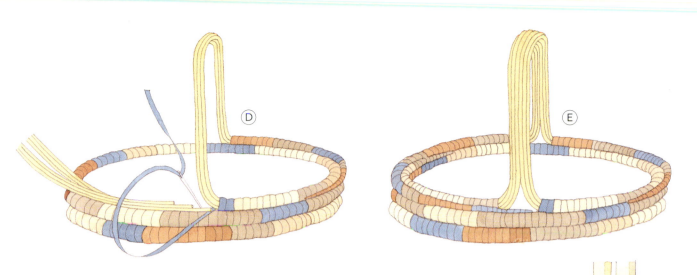

8 Join in six more strands of cane. Stagger their beginnings (D) and bind them around the other half of the basket. Arch the canes over, alongside the first handle bundle and work a final row of coiling to bind the ends to the rim, fading them out in the same way as the first bundle (E).

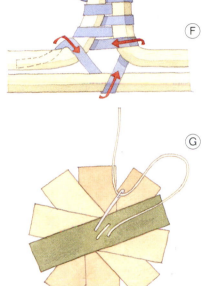

9 Secure the end of a new strip of rag by threading it through three or four stitches of the existing coiling, and work extra stitches over the points where the handle cores meet the rim, as they will take the most strain here (F). Bind as before all the way along the handle. Strengthen the handle join on the other side with a few extra stitches and thread the end of the fabric away into the rim.

10 To decorate the basket with fabric flowers cut out about five small rectangles of the fabric of your choice. Layer them to make a flower-like shape and, with a sewing needle and linen thread, work a couple of large stitches through the center (G). Pull the thread tight to scrunch up the fabric and knot the ends together.

11 Stitch the flowers to the rim of the basket. You can use one long continuous length of thread, using your needle to take it under the coiling in between flowers. Cut leaf shapes out of green felt and sew them on. Finally, apply fabric stiffener to prevent the flowers from fraying.

close-up

Base

Extra stitches where handle meets rim

Rag leaves and roses

diamond pattern
fruit bowl

This little bowl is made from a straw core wrapped with iris leaves and is highlighted with sweet corn husks.

raw materials

Prepare the following leaves and straw according to the instructions on pages 13 and 15:

A couple of handfuls of straw

Generous bundle of iris or other dark colored leaves for wrapping material

Handful of sweet corn husks, natural raffia or other light colored leaves, split along their length if they are thick, for the diamond pattern

other essentials
Large-eyed needle

1 Trap the end of an iris leaf in a bundle of straw (about $\frac{3}{8}$ inch diameter), bind over it and bend the core into a circle (see steps 2–3, page 67).

2 Holding the circle firmly together, start to coil, making navajo stitches into the middle of the circle (see step 3, page 74).

3 Continue in the same way to make a base measuring about 4 inches in diameter. Increase as necessary by working two new stitches into one on the previous round. Add in new straws to maintain the thickness of the core.

4 Gradually form a bowl shape by positioning the core at the desired angle each time you make a new stitch. When the bowl is about $3\frac{1}{2}$ inches deep, start to bring in single stitches with pieces of corn at intervals about $2\frac{1}{4}$ inches apart all round the basket. Join in corn as shown in step 5 on page 69 and thread it into the needle. Bring the

corn to the front to make a stitch before putting it to the back again, under the wrapping (A).

5 On the next round, work three corn stitches above each of the existing ones. Due to their short length it is advisable to join in three new ends securely before the start of each section of diamond, then each one will be ready to use in turn.

6 On the next round work single corn stitches again.

7 Do a round in iris before fading out the coil and making a final round of wraps all the way round the rim.

(A)

close-up

Diamond pattern in navajo stitch   *Fading out the rim*   *Rim and base*

list of suppliers

Allen's Basketworks Inc.
Box 3217 Palm Springs
CA. 92263
basketry@teleport.com
Basket weaving materials

American Baskets & Gifts
Aka MS Creations
22 Roderick Court
Beech Grove
IN 46107-2534
mscreations@bewley.net
Basket weaving materials

Atkinson's Country House
2775 Riniel Road
Lennon, MI 48449
sandy@sandyatkinson.com
Basket weaving materials

A.T. Pettengill Woodworking Co.
PO Box 632, Route 4
Epsom, NH 03234
603-736-8663
Basket bases

Basketry Handle Supply Inc.
1126 Brookside Drive
Lebanon, IN 46052
paulsims@in-motion.net
Basket handles

The Basketmaker's Shop
45 Mutton Road
Webster, NH 03303
Kimball@kear.tds.net
Basket weaving materials

The Basket Shoppe
2205 N. Calhoun Road
Brookfield
WI 53005
friends@thebasketshoppe.com
Basket weaving materials

Basket Werks
27355 Scott Park Road
Long Grove, IA 52756
319-285-4851
Basket weaving materials

Cane and Reed
Box 762
Manchester CT 06040
800-227-8498
Basket weaving materials

The Country Workshops
990 Black Pine Ridge Road
Marshall, NC 28753
828-656-2280
Tools for basket weaving

East Troy Basketry Co.
P.O. Box 643
East Troy
WI 53120
Basket weaving materials

Frank's Cane and Rush Supply
7252 Heil Ave.
Huntington Beach
CA 92647
franks@franksupply.com
Basket weaving materials

Ozark Basketry Supply
P.O. Box 599
Fayetteville
AR 72702
501-442-9292
Basket weaving supplies

Royalwood Ltd.
517 Woodville Road
Mansfield
Ohio 44907
Basket weaving and
caning supplies

The Weaving Works
4717 Brooklyn Ave. NE
Seattle
WA 98105
1-888-524-1221
Basket weaving materials

Willowe's Basketry
226 W. Main st.
Greenfield
IN 46140
800-230-3195
Caning and basket weaving
supplies

Woven Spirit Basketry
635 N. Tamiami Trail
Nokomis
FL 34275
800-697-6730
Basket weaving supplies

bibliography

H.H. Bobart *Basketwork Through The Ages* (Oxford University Press).

Germaine Brotherton *Rush and Leafcraft* (Batsford; ISBN 0 7134 0383 7).

Olivia Elton Barratt *Basketmaking* (Letts and Co; ISBN 1 85238 109 4).

Olivia Elton Barratt *Rushwork* (Dryad Press; ISBN 0 8521 96075).

Fibrearts Vol. 19, No. 1 *The Vessel* (ISBN 0164 324 X)

The Fibre Basketweavers of South Australia *Fibre Basketry* (Kangaroo Press; ISBN 0 86417 265 6).

R. Fitler, A. Fitler and A. Farrer *Grasses, Sedges, Rushes and Ferns* (Harper Collins; ISBN 0 00219136 9).

Sue Gabriel and Sally Goymer *The Complete Book of Basketry Techniques* (David and Charles; ISBN 0 7153 9424 X).

Osma Gallinger Tod *Earth Basketry* (Schiffer; ISBN 0 88740 076 0).

Virginia I Harvey *The Techniques of Basketry* (Batsford; ISBN 0 7134 2977 1).

The Hillier Manual of Trees and Shrubs (David and Charles; ISBN 0 71539942 X).

Marjorie Locke *Basketry Patterns in Matabeleland: The Doves Footprints* (Baobab Books, a division of Academic Books; ISBN 0 908311 74 5).

Richard Mabey *Flora Britannica* (Sinclair Stevenson; ISBN 1 85619 377 2).

John McGuire *Basketry the Nantucket Tradition* (Lark Books; ISBN 0 937274 50 X).

John McGuire *Basketry The Shaker Tradition* (Sterling/Lark Books, ISBN 0 937274 46 1).

Rob Pulleyn (editor) *The Basketmaker's Art, Contemporary Baskets and their Makers* (Lark Books; ISBN 0 937274 63 1).

Mabel Roffey and Charlotte S. Cross *Rush Work* (Sir Isaac Pitman and Sons).

M. Swannell *Coiled Basketry* (George Philip and Son).

M. Swannell *Raffia Work* (George Philip and Son).

Traditional British Crafts (Colour Library Books, prepared by Marshall Cavendish Books Ltd; ISBN 0 86283 753 7).

Susie Vaughan *Handmade Baskets from Nature's Colourful Materials* (Search Press; ISBN 0 85532 755 3).

Lois Walpole *Creative Basketmaking* (Collins; ISBN 0 00 412245 3).

Dorothy Wright *The Complete Book of Baskets and Basketry* (David and Charles; ISBN 0 7153 7449 4).

index

Numbers in italics refer to captions